101 BAR BITES

CHORIZO & RED (BELL) PEPPER FRITTATA BITES

SEE PAGE 126

101
BAR BITES

DELICIOUS NIBBLES, SNACKS & SMALL PLATES
TO COMPLEMENT YOUR DRINKS

RYLAND PETERS & SMALL
LONDON • NEW YORK

First published in 2017 by
Ryland Peters & Small
20–21 Jockey's Fields
London WC1R 4BW
and
341 E 116th St
New York, NY 10029
www.rylandpeters.com

Recipe collection compiled by
Alice Sambrook. Recipe text
© Amy Ruth Finegold, Annie
Rigg, Carol Hilker, Chloe
Coker & Jane Montgomery,
Dan May, Ghillie Basan,
Hannah Miles, Jackie Kearney,
Jennifer Joyce, Jenny Linford,
Milli Taylor, Miranda Ballard,
Shelagh Ryan, Valerie Aikman-
Smith, Uyen Luu and Vicky
Jones.

Design & photography
© Ryland Peters & Small 2017

A CIP catalog record for this
book is available from the
Library of Congress and the
British Library.

ISBN: 978-1-84975-807-9

Printed in China

10 9 8 7 6 5 4 3 2 1

Editor: Alice Sambrook
Designer: Paul Stradling
Production: Mai-Ling Collyer
Editorial Director: Julia Charles
Art Director: Leslie Harrington
Publisher: Cindy Richards

Indexer: Vanessa Bird

NOTES

• Both British (metric) and American (imperial plus US cup) measurements are included; however, its important not to alternate between the two within a recipe.

• All eggs are medium (UK) or large (US), unless otherwise specified. It is recommended that free-range, organic eggs be used whenever possible. Recipes containing raw or partially cooked egg should not be served to the very young, very old, anyone with a compromised immune system or pregnant women.

• When a recipe calls for grated zest of citrus fruit, buy unwaxed fruit and wash well before use. If you can only find treated fruit, scrub and rinse before using.

• Ovens should be preheated to the specified temperatures. All ovens work slightly differently. We recommend using an oven thermometer and suggest you consult the maker's handbook for any special instructions, particularly if you are cooking in a fan-assisted/convection oven, as you may need to adjust temperatures.

CONTENTS

INTRODUCTION

An increasingly popular genre of laid-back eating, bar bites are the perfect choice for peckish revellers who are after something more than a lacklustre nibble but less than a heavy meal. A full meal is great on occasion, but it's not always suitable. It can lull you into a delicious but unsociable food-stupor – rendering you far too full to go out dancing or even hold a slightly up-tempo conversation. It's easy to accidentally spend a fortune on fancy fare after a few drinks, or worst of all be forced to get up from a prime-position bar stool and interrupt the flow of an evening in search of sustenance. A fortifying and delicious bar bite is the answer to these problems! A decent bar bite should bring something to the party, not detract. Its delicious flavours and sharing aspect should make it tempting, easy and just nicely satisfying. Most won't necessarily require a knife and fork, they can often be cheesy, meaty or deep-fried, but they can also be light and sophisticated and everything in between. With this book you can transfer this cool eating concept to your very own cocktail parties, gatherings and cosy nights in. In these pages find bar bites to suit every drink and every occasion.

Find interesting nibbles in *Tasty Titbits* such as Salted Pretzel Bites, Spiced Marinated Olives and North African Roasted Chickpeas. In *Cocktail Canapés* classy bites abound, such as Pea and Pancetta Crostini, Scallop and Chorizo Skewers and Corn Fritter Blinis with Smoked Salmon and Lemon Cream. Up the ante in the *Beer Buddies* chapter with Deep-Fried Mozzarella Cheese Sticks, Jalapeño Poppers and Scotch Quails' Eggs. In *Meaty Munchies* cure those hunger pangs in a flash with Buffalo Chicken Wings, a Steak Sandwich or Pork Belly Bites. *Moreish Mezze* offers treats with a twist like Persian Sausage Rolls, Stuffed Vine Leaves and Lamb kofta Skewers. The snacks in *Fragrant Finger Food* go well with most drinks, from Steamed Vegetable Dumplings to Duck Breast Chinese Pancakes and Salt and Pepper Squid. *Morsels from the Med* contains snacks that just call out for a glass of wine, from Roast Garlic Salt Cod Croquettes to Lemon and Mushroom Risotto Balls. Finally, when you fancy something *Sweet & Neat* try the Churros or the Mini Berry Pavlovas. Because eating is still cheating, but bar bites are ok!

CHAPTER 1

TASTY TITBITS

500 g/5 cups assorted unsalted nuts (cashews, hazelnuts, brazil nuts, peanuts, blanched almonds, pecans, walnuts)

1 tablespoon fennel seeds

2 tablespoons sesame seeds

100 g/¾ cup pumpkin seeds

1½ tablespoons (about 2 sprigs) coarsely chopped rosemary

1 teaspoon chilli/hot red pepper flakes

4 teaspoons dark muscovado sugar

1 teaspoon sea salt

2 tablespoons melted unsalted butter

serves 4

SPICED MIXED NUTS

SPICED MIXED NUTS WITH FRESHLY MADE COCKTAILS ARE AN INDULGENT TREAT ON A LAZY SUMMER AFTERNOON OR LONG WARM EVENING. THEY WILL KEEP YOU GOING UNTIL DINNER BUT BE WARNED THEY ARE INCREDIBLY MOREISH! YOU MAY WANT TO KEEP THEM HIDDEN IN A CUPBOARD BEFORE GUESTS ARRIVE TO STOP YOURSELF FROM CONSTANTLY NIBBLING AWAY.

★ Preheat the oven to 180°C (350°F) Gas 4.

★ Mix the nuts together in a bowl and then spread on a non-stick baking sheet.

★ Toast in the preheated oven for about 10 minutes, until lightly golden brown. Keep a close eye on them though as the nuts can burn quickly.

★ Meanwhile, put the fennel, sesame and pumpkin seeds in a preheated frying pan/skillet set over a medium heat. Dry fry the seeds for a few minutes until the sesame seeds turn lightly golden brown.

★ Put the rosemary, chilli/hot red pepper flakes, sugar, salt and melted butter in a large mixing bowl and stir to combine.

★ While the nuts and seeds are still warm from the oven and pan, toss in the butter spice mixture to coat thoroughly.

HARD-BOILED EGGS WITH DUKKAH

100 g/1 cup hazelnuts

20 g/¼ cup pistachio nuts

2 tablespoons coriander seeds

1 tablespoon cumin seeds

40 g/5 tablespoons sesame seeds

2 teaspoons white or black peppercorns

½ teaspoon chilli/hot red pepper flakes

½ teaspoon sea salt

8–10 eggs, to serve

serves 4

DUKKAH IS AN EGYPTIAN DRY SPICE BLEND WITH MANY USES, INCLUDING AS A SEASONING FOR LAMB CHOPS, OR AS A DIP WITH BREAD AND OLIVE OIL. HERE IT IS A LOVELY ACCOMPANIMENT TO HARD-BOILED EGGS.

★ Preheat the oven to 170°C (325°F) Gas 3.

★ Put the hazelnuts and pistachio nuts on separate non-stick baking sheets and roast in the preheated oven for 10 minutes.

★ Remove from the oven and immediately wrap the hazelnuts in a tea/dish towel. Set aside to allow the steam to build for a minute before rubbing the hazelnuts within the tea/dish towel to remove the loose skins. When both the pistachio nuts and hazelnuts are cool, roughly crush them in a pestle and mortar to a chunky texture. Transfer the mixture to a large mixing bowl.

★ Put the coriander and cumin seeds in a preheated frying pan/skillet set over a medium heat. Dry fry the seeds for a couple of minutes, shaking the pan from time to time, until they start to pop. Remove the seeds from the pan and crush in a pestle and mortar. Add to the nuts in the mixing bowl.

★ Put the sesame seeds in the same, dry pan and toast until lightly golden, giving the pan a shake every 30 seconds. Remove from the pan and grind in the pestle and mortar. Add to the nut and seed mixture. Repeat this process with the white or black peppercorns.

★ Lightly grind the chilli/hot red pepper flakes in the pestle and mortar and add to the nut and seed mixture. Add the salt and mix everything together well.

★ Put the eggs in a saucepan with enough cold water to cover by 2.5cm/1 inch. Set over a medium–high heat and bring the water to a boil. As soon as it reaches boil, reduce the heat and simmer for 7 minutes. Take the pan off the heat, discard the water and rinse under cold, running water for 1 minute. Set the eggs aside to cool completely in the pan filled with cold water.

★ Peel the eggs and dip the tops in the dukkah. They're delicious!

SPICY POPCORN

WHAT COULD MAKE A MORE PERFECT EVENING THAN A MOVIE WITH POSH POPCORN AND A GLASS OF WINE? THIS POPCORN HAS A FABULOUS PINK TINT AND SPICY KICK.

4 tablespoons Murray River salt flakes
2 tablespoons chipotle chilli/chili powder, or to taste
2 bags unsalted microwave popcorn

serves 4

★ In a small bowl, mix together the salt and chilli/chili powder.

★ Cook the popcorn according to the instructions on the packet. When it has popped, put in a large bowl, sprinkle with the chilli/chili salt and toss to mix.

GOLD TRUFFLED POTATO CHIPS

POTATOES, TRUFFLES AND SALT ARE A MATCH MADE IN HEAVEN. USE A MANDOLIN TO SLICE THE POTATOES WAFER THIN.

450 g/1 lb. Mayan Gold potatoes or similar (about 6 small), skin on
vegetable oil, for deep-frying
truffle salt, to sprinkle

an electric deep-fat fryer (optional)
a deep-frying thermometer

serves 4–6

★ Wash and dry the potatoes, slice thinly and set aside.

★ Heat the oil in the deep–fat fryer or a heavy-bottom pan until it reaches 180°C (350°F). To test if the oil is hot enough, drop a cube of bread in the oil – it should turn golden brown in about 20 seconds.

★ Fry the potato slices in batches and drain on paper towels.

★ Put the drained potato chips in a bowl, sprinkle with the truffle salt, toss and serve.

PADRÓN PEPPERS

ONE IN EVERY DOZEN PADRÓN PEPPERS HAS A FIERY HIT, SO BE PREPARED WITH YOUR GLASS OF COLD BEER TO HAND.

60 ml/¼ cup olive oil
450 g/1 lb. Padrón peppers
sel gris, or other coarse sea salt, to sprinkle

serves 4–6

★ Put a frying pan/skillet over a high heat. When it starts to smoke, turn the heat down to medium. Add the olive oil and swirl the pan once to cover the bottom with oil.

★ Add the peppers and cook until slightly blistered, stirring occasionally. Empty the hot peppers into a bowl and sprinkle generously with the sel gris.

CORSICAN OLIVES

115 g/4 oz. goats' cheese, room temperature

1 teaspoon herbes de Provence

finely grated zest of 1 orange

1 egg

1 tablespoon plain/all-purpose flour

60 g/1 cup panko breadcrumbs

40 large green and black olives, pitted/stoned

500 ml/2 cups vegetable oil

sea salt to sprinkle

a piping/pastry bag with a small nozzle/tip

a deep-frying thermometer

makes 40

★ In a bowl, mix the goats' cheese, herbs and zest until smooth and put it in the piping bag. Set aside.

★ Lightly beat the egg in a small bowl and set aside. Put the flour and breadcrumbs on two separate plates.

★ Using the piping bag, pipe each olive full with the cheese mixture. Dip each olive in the flour, then the egg and toss in the breadcrumbs.

★ Heat the oil in a heavy-bottom pan until the oil reaches 180°C (350°F). Fry the olives in batches until golden brown, about 1 minute. Drain on paper towels. Sprinkle with sea salt and serve.

CANDIED SALTED ALMONDS

270 g/2 cups raw almonds, skin on

60 g/½ cup dark brown sugar

60 g/½ cup maple syrup

1 teaspoon chipotle chilli/chili powder

1 tablespoon sel gris, coarsely ground

makes 400 g/2 cups

★ Preheat the oven to 190°C (375°F) Gas 5.

★ Mix all the ingredients except for the sel gris together in a bowl until the almonds are well coated. Spread the almonds on a non-stick baking sheet and bake in the preheated oven for 5–8 minutes. The sugars will bubble and turn a darker colour.

★ Remove the almonds from the oven and stir with a wooden spoon. Sprinkle with sel gris and set aside to cool on the baking sheet. As they cool, the sugars will harden.

★ When the almonds have cooled, serve them in a bowl. They can be stored in an airtight container for a week at room temperature.

SPICED & MARINATED OLIVES

1 dried red chilli/chile

90 g/¼ cup Spanish salted Marcona almonds

170 g/1 cup green olives

3 kumquats

½ teaspoon cumin seeds

60 ml/¼ cup olive oil

makes 400 g/2 cups

★ Roughly chop the chilli/chile and the almonds and put them in a bowl with the olives.

★ Thinly slice the kumquats and add to the olive mixture.

★ Sprinkle with cumin seeds, pour over the olive oil and mix thoroughly. Set aside for at least 1 hour before serving to let the flavours blend.

THESE SAVOURY BITES ARE THE PERFECT ACCOMPANIMENT TO MOST DRINKS. A SPRINKLE OF HIMALAYAN PINK ROCK SALT TO FINISH IS AN EASY WAY OF ADDING INTEREST TO PLAIN SNACKS.

SALTED PRETZEL BITES

250 ml/1 cup warm water

2 tablespoons salted butter, room temperature, in small cubes

3 teaspoons fast-action dried yeast

1 teaspoon white sugar

400 g/2¾ cups plain/all-purpose flour

4 teaspoons baking powder

rock salt flakes, for topping

American mustard, to serve (optional)

makes about 40

★ In a glass measuring jug, mix together the warm water, butter, yeast and sugar. Stir until the butter has melted.

★ Put the flour in a food processor and add the liquid in a steady stream until the dough forms a ball, about 3 minutes. Knead on a floured work surface for 2 minutes. Put the ball of dough in an oiled bowl. Cover with a tea/dish towel and leave to prove in a warm place for 1 hour.

★ Preheat the oven to 220°C (425°F) Gas 7.

★ Turn the dough out onto a floured worktop and roll into a 30 x 15-cm/12 x 6-inch rectangle. With a sharp knife, cut 2.5-cm/1-inch strips of dough from the long side. Cut into 2.5-cm/1-inch bite-sized pieces.

★ In a non-stick pan (do not use aluminium), bring the baking powder to a boil with 1 litre/4 cups water. Drop the dough pieces into the water for about 1 minute and remove with a slotted spoon onto non-stick baking sheets.

★ Sprinkle over the rock salt and bake in the preheated oven for 10–15 minutes until brown on top. Serve with American mustard, if desired.

PARMESAN & SAGE WAFERS

110 g/1 cup freshly grated Parmesan

1 tablespoon finely chopped fresh sage

freshly ground black pepper

Himalayan pink rock salt

makes 14

★ Preheat the oven to 180°C (350°F) Gas 4.

★ Mix together the Parmesan and sage and season with black pepper. Drop tablespoons of the mixture at 5-cm/2-inch intervals on a non-stick baking sheet. Pat down the mounds with your fingers. Bake in the preheated oven for 5–6 minutes until the mixture is completely melted and the edges are turning golden brown. Keep an eye on them as they brown fast.

★ Remove the wafers from the oven and set aside for a few moments to firm up. They will be soft when they come out of the oven but will harden as they cool.

★ With a spatula, carefully remove the wafers and arrange on a wire rack to cool completely. Once cooled, sprinkle with Himalayan rock salt. The wafers can be stored in an airtight container for 2 days. These delicate lacy wafers are ideal with a glass of prosecco.

EXTRA-LONG HAWAIIAN BLACK SALTED BREADSTICKS

450 g/3½ cups plain/all-purpose flour

300 ml/1⅓ cups warm water

3 tablespoons olive oil

1 tablespoon milk

3 teaspoons fast-action dried yeast

½ teaspoon brown sugar

60 ml/¼ cup olive oil, for brushing

110 g/¼ cup Hawaiian black lava salt

makes about 24

THESE MOREISH TREATS ARE SPRINKLED WITH HAWAIIAN BLACK LAVA SALT. ITS DISTINCTIVE INKY COLOUR IS THE PRODUCT OF REMNANTS OF ACTIVATED CHARCOAL FROM HAWAIIAN VOLCANOES.

★ To make the dough, put the flour in a food processor. Mix together the warm water, olive oil, milk, yeast and brown sugar in a glass measuring jug. With the motor running, add the liquid to the flour in a steady stream. Process until all the liquid is incorporated and the dough forms a ball, about 3 minutes.

★ Transfer the dough to a floured work surface and knead for about 3 minutes. Form into a ball and put in an oiled bowl. Cover with a tea/dish towel and leave to prove in a warm place until it doubles in size.

★ Preheat the oven to 220°C (425°F) Gas 7.

★ Turn the dough out onto a floured work surface. Roll it into a rectangle measuring 25 x 40 cm/15 x 10 inches, and 5-mm/¼-inch thick. Use a sharp knife to cut 1-cm/½-inch strips of dough from the long side of the rectangle. Fold the strips in half and with the palms of your hands roll the dough into breadsticks measuring 25 cm/10 inches.

★ Arrange the breadsticks on non-stick baking sheets. Brush with olive oil and sprinkle with the Hawaiian black lava salt.

★ Bake in the preheated oven for 10 minutes, turn the sticks over, and bake for another 10 minutes until golden. Leave to cool on a wire rack.

CHICKPEA FRITTERS

IN SICILY, CHICKPEA/GRAM FLOUR IS BOILED WITH WATER TO MAKE A THICK BATTER,
ALLOWED TO COOL, THEN CUT INTO SQUARES AND FRIED INTO IRRESISTIBLE SOFT-YET-
CRUNCHY FRITTERS CALLED PANELLE. BEST EATEN HOT, THEY MAKE A SOPHISTICATED
AND MORE SATISFYING ALTERNATIVE TO SERVING CRISPS/POTATO CHIPS WITH DRINKS.
THE DOUGH CAN ALSO BE CUT INTO SQUARES OR BATONS, IF PREFERRED.

250 g/2 cups chickpea/gram flour, sifted

1 teaspoon sea salt

1 tablespoon freshly chopped flat-leaf parsley

3 tablespoons olive oil

coarse sea salt and freshly ground black pepper

serves 4–6

★ Whisk the chickpea/gram flour into 1 litre/4 cups of water until there are no lumps, then season with the salt.

★ Heat the batter gently in a saucepan, stirring constantly, until it boils and thickens. Simmer the mixture for about 15 minutes, whisking constantly, as lumps tend to form otherwise. Stir in the parsley and cook for another 5 minutes.

★ Pour the batter into an oiled baking sheet about 30 x 20 cm (12 x 8 inches), and smooth out the surface. The mixture should be no more than 1-cm/½-inch thick. Leave to cool for several hours to allow the mixture to solidify.

★ Preheat the oven to 200°C (400°F) Gas 6. When the batter has cooled and solidified, cut it into triangles, squares or, to make chunky chips, batons about the size of your largest finger.

★ When the oven is hot, put the olive oil in a clean baking sheet and heat in the oven for a few minutes, then using a spatula, transfer the triangles, squares or batons to the hot oil, flipping over once to coat both sides with oil. Put in the oven for about 20 minutes, until the panelle are crisp on the surface and starting to brown, then turn over and cook for another 10 minutes.

★ Alternatively, heat some oil in a frying pan/skillet, and fry the panelle on the hob/stovetop.

★ Sprinkle with coarse sea salt and black pepper and serve immediately.

HARICOTS VERTS TEMPURA

TEMPURA GREEN BEANS DUSTED WITH HACHIMI TOGARASHI IS A MATCH MADE IN HEAVEN.

200 g/1½ cups rice flour

½ teaspoon ground Hachimi Togarashi peppermill mix, plus extra for dusting

½ teaspoon sea salt

1 egg

350 ml/1¼ cups soda water/club soda

vegetable oil, for frying

450 g/1 lb. haricots verts, trimmed

serves 4

★ Put all the ingredients except the oil and haricots verts in a blender and process for about 30 seconds until mixed, then pour into a shallow bowl.

★ Pour enough oil to come halfway up a wide medium-sized saucepan, then set over a medium–high heat until the oil starts to simmer.

★ Working in batches, dip the beans in the batter and deep fry for 3–4 minutes until golden and cooked. Transfer to a wire rack to drain, dust with Hachimi Togarashi and serve.

NORTH AFRICAN ROASTED CHICKPEAS

SPICY AND CRUNCHY, YOU WON'T BE ABLE TO STOP EATING THIS BITE-SIZE SNACK.

1 tablespoon harissa paste

1 tablespoon extra virgin olive oil

1 teaspoon cracked smoked peppercorns

1 teaspoon ground coriander

1 teaspoon ground cumin

1 teaspoon sea salt

2 x 400-g/14-oz. cans chickpeas, drained and rinsed

serves 6–10

★ Preheat the oven to 200°C (400°F) Gas 6.

★ In a bowl whisk together the harissa, oil, pepper, coriander, cumin and salt until combined. Add the chickpeas and toss to coat.

★ Spread the chickpeas out in an even layer on a non-stick baking sheet and roast in the preheated oven for 30 minutes. Shake the pan halfway through cooking. Remove from the oven and cool before serving. Store in an airtight container for up to 1 week.

'STREET HAWKER' TEA EGGS

SOLD AS STREET FOOD IN CHINA, THESE EGGS MAKE A FUN ADDITION TO A CHINESE FEAST.

6 eggs, hard-boiled

1 black tea bag

4 star anise

1 teaspoon five-spice powder, plus extra to serve

2 teaspoons cracked Szechuan pepper

1 cinnamon stick

120 ml/½ cup soy sauce

sea salt, to serve

makes 6

★ Gently roll the eggs on a work surface to crack the eggshells all over.

★ Put the remaining ingredients except those to serve into a pan and pour over 475 ml/2 cups of water. Bring to the boil over a high heat, then reduce to a simmer and cook for 5 minutes.

★ Remove from the heat and add the eggs to the pan. Let the liquid cool, then refrigerate overnight.

★ Remove the eggs from the liquid and peel. Cut in half and sprinkle with salt and extra five-spice mix.

SPICY DILL PICKLES

PICKLES ARE A STAPLE AROUND THE GLOBE, AND THEY ARE NEVER MORE DELICIOUS THAN AS A TASTY BAR SNACK. THESE THREE PICKLES WILL KEEP FOR UP TO TWO WEEKS IN THE REFRIGERATOR.

300 ml/1¼ cups white vinegar

3 tablespoons sea salt

675 g/24 oz. pickling cucumbers, quartered or halved and sliced lengthways

8 fresh dill sprigs

8 large garlic cloves

4 dried hot chilli/chile peppers

4 x sterilized 450-ml/16-oz. canning jars

makes 4 jars

★ In a stainless steel stockpot, bring 1 litre/4 cups water, vinegar and salt to a boil and let boil for 10–12 minutes.

★ Meanwhile, pack the cucumbers facing upwards into canning jars. Ensure they are at least 1 cm/ ½ inch below the jar's rim. Place 2 dill sprigs, 2 garlic cloves and 1 chilli/chile pepper in each jar. Carefully ladle the hot mixture into the jars. Add extra water if necessary so that the cucumbers are submerged, but leave 1 cm/ ½ inch of space from the rim of the jar. Remove air bubbles, wipe the rims and put the lids on. Let the cucumbers pickle for at least 24 hours before tasting.

SWEET PICKLES

240 ml/1 cup cider vinegar

40 g/⅛ cup sea salt

200 g/1 cup granulated sugar

¼ teaspoon ground turmeric

½ teaspoon mustard seeds

400 g/14 oz. pickling cucumbers, quartered or halved and sliced lengthways

1 sweet onion, sliced

2 x sterilized 450-ml/16-oz. canning jars

makes 2 jars

★ In a small saucepan over a medium–high heat, combine the cider vinegar, salt, sugar, turmeric and mustard seeds. Bring to a boil and cook for 5 minutes.

★ Loosely pack the cucumbers and the onion into canning jars and pour the hot liquid over them. Remove air bubbles, wipe the rims and put the lids on. Let the cucumbers pickle for at least 24 hours before tasting.

SWEET & SOUR CHERRY PICKLES

½ jar Spicy Dill Pickles (see left), including the brine

1 packet cherry Kool-Aid powder

200 g/1 cup granulated sugar

1 x sterilized 450-ml/16-oz. canning jar

makes 1 jar

★ Follow the recipe to the left for Spicy Dill Pickles.

★ After the brining is done, remove the pickles from the liquid. Stir in the sugar and the Kool-Aid to the pickle brine until they have both dissolved. Add the pickles back to the mixture, and seal in the jar. Place in the refrigerator and let pickle for at least 1 week before tasting.

PEA & PANCETTA CROSTINI

NOTHING COULD BE SIMPLER THAN PUTTING TOGETHER THESE TEMPTING TOASTS, THEY MAKE THE PERFECT SOPHISTICATED LIGHT BITE.

10 slices/strips pancetta

300 g/2¼ cups frozen petits pois

200 g/1¼ cups broad/fava beans, fresh or frozen

1 tablespoon olive oil

grated zest of ½ lemon

100 g/3½ oz. ricotta

10 freshly chopped mint leaves, plus 10 leaves, to garnish

sea salt and freshly ground black pepper

40 thin baguette slices, brushed with olive oil

200 g/7 oz. feta, crumbled

makes 40

★ Preheat the oven to 180°C (350°F) Gas 4.

★ Cut each slice/strip of pancetta crossways into 4 pieces. Put the pancetta onto a non-stick baking sheet and bake in the preheated oven for 10 minutes, or until crisp. Drain any excess fat on paper towels and set aside.

★ Put the frozen petits pois in a pan of boiling water for 1 minute and then immediately plunge into cold water. Repeat with the beans and then squeeze them out of their skins.

★ Put the petits pois and half of the beans into a food processor or blender. Blend together with the olive oil, lemon zest, ricotta, mint, salt and pepper.

★ Heat a griddle pan and cook the baguette slices, in batches, for 1 minute on each side until toasted.

★ Spread a teaspoonful of the mix on top of each crostini, followed by a little feta, chopped mint, remaining beans and piece of pancetta. Serve.

PESTO VEGETABLE CROSTINI

SPREAD GENEROUSLY WITH DELICIOUS FRESH PESTO, THESE WILL WORK WELL WITH MOST VEGETABLES.

4 tablespoons olive oil

1 red/bell pepper

½ aubergine/eggplant, thinly sliced

1 courgette/zucchini, thinly sliced

¼ red onion, cut into wedges (optional)

1 x 125-g/4½-oz. mozzarella ball

40 thin baguette slices, brushed with olive oil

for the pesto

50 g/generous ⅓ cup pine nuts

40 g/1½ oz. fresh basil leaves

1 garlic clove

60 g/1 cup freshly grated Parmesan

3 tablespoons olive oil

a squeeze of lemon juice

freshly ground black pepper

makes 40

★ Preheat the oven to 200°C (400°F) Gas 6.

★ To make the pesto, toast the pine nuts in a dry frying pan/skillet, stirring regularly. Blitz in a food processor with the rest of the pesto ingredients until smooth. Set aside.

★ Rub a little olive oil onto the red/bell pepper and roast in the preheated oven until the skin blisters and turns black. Remove from the oven, wrap in foil and, when cool enough, remove the skin. Slice into thin strips.

★ Brush the aubergine/eggplant and courgette/zucchini with oil and grill/broil for 2–3 minutes on each side. Do the same with the red onion, if using. Divide the mozzarella into quarters, then divide each quarter into 10.

★ Heat a griddle pan and cook the baguette slices, in batches, for 1 minute on each side until toasted.

★ Spread half a teaspoon of pesto onto each crostini. Top with mozzarella, the vegetables and black pepper. Serve.

CHORIZO & SCALLOP SKEWERS

THIS IS AS LOVELY A COMBINATION OF TEXTURES AS IT IS OF FLAVOURS. THE SCALLOPS BECOME SLIGHTLY PINK AS THEY BECOME GENTLY INFUSED WITH THE RICH CHORIZO OIL, AND THE SMOKY TASTE OF PAPRIKA PERMEATES THE SOFT FLESH. THIS RECIPE CAN BE MADE USING EITHER FRESH OR FROZEN SCALLOPS. FROZEN ONES COOK BEAUTIFULLY AND ARE GREAT TO HAVE ON STAND-BY. GIVEN THAT CHORIZO HAS SUCH A LOVELY LONG SHELF-LIFE, HAVING A BAG OF FROZEN SCALLOPS TO HAND MEANS THAT YOU CAN QUICKLY AND EASILY WHIP UP THIS CANAPÉ WITHOUT EVEN HAVING TO LEAVE THE HOUSE.

12 shelled scallops (or frozen scallops, defrosted)

chorizo, cut into 12 x 1-cm/½-inch cubes

sea salt and freshly ground black or pink pepper

olive oil, for frying

smoked paprika, for sprinkling

cocktail sticks/toothpicks

makes 12

★ First, fry the scallops in a little olive oil in a frying pan/skillet over high heat for 1 minute on each side, until cooked. Add a good grinding of pepper, then add the chorizo cubes and fry for a further 2–3 minutes, turning and stirring everything often.

★ Remove the chorizo and scallops from the pan, and leave until cool enough to handle, then thread one scallop and chorizo cube onto a cocktail stick/toothpick. Put the scallop on first as the chorizo does a better job of gripping the stick.

★ Repeat to make 12 canapés in total. Serve immediately, while still warm, sprinkled with a little smoked paprika, if you like.

★ **Variation:** You can always add a little chilli/chili powder or smoked paprika to coat the scallops before cooking, but you may find that enough flavourful oil comes out of good-quality chorizo as you fry it.

'SUSHI-STYLE' PROSCIUTTO-WRAPPED GOATS' CHEESE & ROCKET/ARUGULA

INSPIRED BY THE SHAPE OF JAPANESE 'NORI' ROLLS, THIS COMBINATION OF CREAMY GOATS' CHEESE AND PEPPERY ROCKET/ARUGULA ENCASED IN A SALTY SPHERE OF PROSCIUTTO MAKES FOR A MAGICAL MORSEL. UNLIKE NORI ROLLS, HOWEVER, WHICH ARE KEPT TOGETHER WITH THEIR SEAWEED CASING, YOU WILL NEED COCKTAIL STICKS/ TOOTHPICKS TO ENSURE THEY DON'T FALL APART. A BLUE CHEESE, SUCH AS GORGONZOLA, IS A GREAT ALTERNATIVE TO GOATS' CHEESE FOR A SHARPER FLAVOUR.

12 slices prosciutto

24 teaspoons olive tapenade

a handful of rocket/arugula (about 4–5 leaves per roll)

200 g/7 oz. goats' cheese, sliced into 12 strips (or cheese of your choice; Gorgonzola is good too)

cocktail sticks/toothpicks

makes 24

★ Lay a slice of prosciutto flat on a board or plate. Spread 1 teaspoon of the olive tapenade over the surface. Sprinkle 4–5 rocket/arugula leaves on the top, then put a strip of cheese on top in the middle.

★ Roll the prosciutto over on itself to enclose the filling, like a 'nori' roll, and then slice (it is easiest to snip with kitchen scissors) in half to create two circles. Push a cocktail stick/toothpick through each assembled bite to hold it together.

★ Repeat to make 24 bites in total. Serve immediately.

★ Alternatively, roll each slice of prosciutto with its filling into a cone so it's wider at the top, like 'temaki'. You will make 12 larger bites using this method.

CORNICHONS WRAPPED IN SALAMI

AS SIMPLE AS THE NAME SUGGESTS. THESE MINI GHERKINS ARE OFTEN SERVED WITH SALAMI BECAUSE THE FLAVOURS COMPLEMENT EACH OTHER PERFECTLY. THIS COMBINATION REALLY IS A DELIGHT FOR THE TASTEBUDS – SALTINESS FROM THE MEAT AND ACIDITY OF THE PICKLED CORNICHONS. IF YOU PUT THEM SIDE BY SIDE ON THE SERVING PLATE, NOBODY CAN RESIST ROLLING THEM UP, SO YOU MIGHT AS WELL DO THE WORK FOR THEM!

12 slices salami
12 cornichons (or 12 small slices of pickled gherkin)
freshly ground black pepper

cocktail sticks/toothpicks

makes 12

★ For each bite, just wrap a slice of salami around a cornichon and pop a cocktail stick/toothpick through the middle to hold them together.

★ Repeat to make 12 bites in total. Crack a little pepper over the plate and serve.

MOZZARELLA PEARLS WRAPPED IN PROSCIUTTO

SO EASY, JUST LIKE THE RECIPE TO THE LEFT. DON'T USE A WHOLE SLICE OF PROSCIUTTO PER MINI MOZZARELLA PEARL/BALL, AS THAT'S A HEAVY MOUTHFUL, AS WELL AS BEING EXPENSIVE FOR ENTERTAINING. USE KITCHEN SCISSORS TO CUT EACH SLICE OF PROSCIUTTO INTO QUARTERS.

3 slices prosciutto
12 mini mozzarella pearls/balls
freshly ground black pepper

cocktail sticks/toothpicks

makes 12

★ Cut each slice of prosciutto lengthways in quarters (kitchen scissors are best for doing this) to make 12 strips in total. Wrap each strip around a mini mozzarella pearl/ball.

★ Pop a cocktail stick/toothpick through the middle of each assembled bite to hold it together, crack a little black pepper over the plate and serve.

DEVILS ON HORSEBACK

THESE ADDICTIVE SALTY AND SWEET BITES ARE GREAT AT ANY TIME OF YEAR.

6 slices prosciutto
12 whole blanched almonds
12 stoned/pitted dried dates or prunes

cocktail sticks/toothpicks

makes 12

★ Cut each slice of prosciutto lengthways down the middle (kitchen scissors work best for doing this) to make 12 half-slices.

★ For each 'devil', put an almond in the middle of a date, wrap a half slice of prosciutto tightly around the fruit and then lay it on a baking sheet. Repeat to make 12 'devils' in total.

★ Preheat the grill/broiler to high.

★ Grill/broil the 'devils' for about 5 minutes, until the prosciutto starts to brown and crisp. Turn the 'devils' over and grill/broil for a further 2–3 minutes. Push a cocktail stick/toothpick through the middle of each one and serve.

HORSES ON DEVILBACK

HUH? HORSES ON DEVILBACK? YES, FAIR'S FAIR. IT'S THE HORSE'S TURN NOW.

12 stoned/pitted prunes
12 slices saucisson sec or 6 slices Serrano ham
6 teaspoons mango chutney

cocktail sticks/toothpicks

makes 12

★ Make sure all the stoned/pitted prunes have holes that run all the way through the middle. If using Serrano ham, cut each slice in half lengthways to make 12 half-slices.

★ For each 'horse', take a slice of saucisson sec or a half-slice of Serrano ham. Spread ½ teaspoon mango chutney over each slice of meat, then roll into tight tubes and thread through the middle of a prune. Lay it on a baking sheet. Repeat to make 12 'horses' in total.

★ Preheat the grill/broiler to high.

★ Grill/broil the 'horses' for about 2 minutes to warm them through, turning once. Push a cocktail stick/toothpick through the middle of each one and serve.

ANGELS ON HORSEBACK

THE MANGO CHUTNEY IS A WORTHWHILE ADDITION TO THESE PARTY FAVOURITES.

6 slices prosciutto
6 teaspoons mango chutney (optional)
12 smoked oysters

cocktail sticks/toothpicks

makes 12

★ Cut each slice of prosciutto lengthways down the middle to make 12 half-slices in total.

★ Spread ½ teaspoon mango chutney at one end of a half-slice of prosciutto. Place a smoked oyster on top and roll up the prosciutto around the oyster. Repeat to make 12 'angels' in total.

★ Heat a non-stick frying pan/skillet over a medium heat. Add the 'angels' to the pan. Cook them over medium heat for 1 minute, then turn over and cook for 1 minute more. This is merely to warm them through and release the flavours.

★ Push a cocktail stick/toothpick through the middle of each one and serve.

POLENTA TART WITH GOATS' CHEESE & TOMATOES

GOATS' CHEESE, CHERRY TOMATOES AND FRESH BASIL ARE A CLASSIC COMBINATION, AND THE BED OF BAKED POLENTA MAKES FOR A TASTY AND USEFUL LITTLE 'PLATE'. THESE ARE DELICIOUS SERVED WITH AN EQUALLY LIGHT AND SUMMERY GIN COCKTAIL.

170 g/1 cup polenta/fine cornmeal

1 tablespoon butter (optional)

1 teaspoon sea salt

1 teaspoon freshly ground black pepper

for the topping

300 g/1 cup cherry tomatoes

1½ teaspoons sea salt

1½ teaspoons freshly ground black pepper

1 tablespoon olive oil

150 g/6 oz. goats' cheese

a handful of fresh basil leaves, to garnish

a rectangular baking sheet, greased

serves 4–6

★ For the topping, cut the tomatoes in half and mix together with the salt, pepper and olive oil. Set aside.

★ Preheat the oven to 180°C (350°F) Gas 4.

★ Bring 1 litre/4 cups water to a boil in a large saucepan or pot, then slowly pour in the polenta while whisking. Whisk for five minutes until fully combined. Reduce the heat, then cover and cook for 15 minutes, stirring vigorously every 5 minutes. Remove the lid, then add a tablespoon of butter, if desired, and the salt and pepper. Stir together then pour onto the prepared baking sheet and bake in the preheated oven for 20 minutes.

★ Remove from the oven and allow to cool completely before cutting into square portions of equal size.

★ Put some of the tomato topping on each square and sprinkle with a little goats' cheese. Garnish with torn fresh basil and season with a little extra salt and pepper, then serve immediately.

TUNA EMPANADAS

- -

THESE DELICIOUS EMPANADAS ARE A POPULAR SNACK IN CENTRAL AND SOUTH AMERICA.

½ tablespoon olive oil

1 garlic clove, finely chopped

½ onion, peeled and diced

200 g/7 oz. tomatoes, scalded, peeled, pulp discarded and shells diced

200 g/7 oz. canned tuna in oil, drained and flaked

2 tablespoons tomato purée/paste

a pinch of chilli/chili powder

½ teaspoon ground cumin

sea salt and freshly ground black pepper,

vegetable oil, for frying

for the pastry

450 g/3½ cups plain/all-purpose flour

2 teaspoons baking powder

1 teaspoon sea salt

60 g/4 tablespoons each of lard and butter, diced

a 7.5-cm/3¼-inch cookie cutter

makes 20

★ Combine the dry ingredients for the pastry in a mixing bowl. Rub in the lard/butter with your fingertips. Slowly add 4–6 tablespoons cold water and bring together to form a dough. Wrap in clingfilm/plastic wrap and chill for 1 hour.

★ Meanwhile, prepare the filling. In a frying pan/skillet, cook the garlic and onion in the olive oil until softened. Add the chopped tomato and fry for 5 minutes, stirring. Mix in the tuna, tomato purée/paste, chilli/chili powder and cumin, and season. Cook for 1–2 minutes.

★ Roll out the pastry on a lightly floured surface and cut out 20 circles using the cookie cutter. Place a teaspoon of the filling in the centre of each circle, brush the edges with water and fold over, pressing together to form little pasties.

★ Heat the vegetable oil in a large frying pan/skillet. Fry the empanadas until lightly browned all over. Remove using a slotted spoon, drain on paper towels and serve.

SMOKED MACKEREL CHERRY TOMATOES

- -

THESE SMALL FILLED CHERRY TOMATO HALVES LOOK AND TASTE FANTASTIC. THE SALTY MACKEREL COMPLEMENTS THE SWEET YET TANGY TOMATO BEAUTIFULLY.

1 smoked mackerel fillet (about 70 g/2½ oz.), skinned

1 tablespoon creamed horseradish sauce

1 tablespoon crème fraîche or sour cream

freshly ground black pepper

14 cherry tomatoes

finely chopped fresh parsley, to garnish

makes 28

★ In a food processor, blend together the smoked mackerel, horseradish sauce and crème fraîche to form a pâté. Season with black pepper. Cover and chill for at least 30 minutes.

★ Next, prepare the tomatoes. Cut them in half and, using a teaspoon, carefully scoop out the soft pulp and seeds, creating 28 cherry tomato shells.

★ Fill each shell with the chilled smoked mackerel pâté. Return to the refrigerator until you are ready to serve. Sprinkle with parsley and serve fridge-cold.

CORN FRITTER BLINIS
with smoked salmon & lemon cream

225 g/2 cups (about 1 medium) grated courgette/zucchini

4 eggs

180 g/1⅓ cups self-raising/rising flour

50 g/1¾ oz. freshly grated Parmesan

100 ml/scant ½ cup buttermilk

1 teaspoon smoked paprika

½ teaspoon cayenne pepper

1 tablespoon freshly chopped coriander/cilantro

fresh corn kernels cut from 2–3 cobs

sunflower oil, for frying

sea salt and freshly ground black pepper, to season

300 g/1½ cups smoked salmon, to serve

chervil or freshly chopped chives, to garnish

for the lemon cream

250 ml/1 cup sour cream

1 tablespoon freshly squeezed lemon juice

1 teaspoon grated lemon zest

¼ teaspoon sea salt

makes 30–35 (serves 10–15)

CORN GIVES A SLIGHT TWIST ON THE TRADITIONAL SMOKED SALMON BLINI. THESE CAN BE MADE AHEAD OF TIME BUT ASSEMBLE JUST BEFORE SERVING. PERFECT WITH A CHAMPAGNE COCKTAIL.

★ Put the grated courgette/zucchini into a colander set over a large mixing bowl. Sprinkle with ½ teaspoon of salt and leave for 30–60 minutes so they release their moisture. Squeeze the grated courgette/zucchini with your hands to get rid of as much moisture as possible and set aside.

★ In a large, clean, dry mixing bowl, lightly whisk the eggs. Add the flour, grated Parmesan, buttermilk, smoked paprika, cayenne pepper, ½ teaspoon of salt, black pepper and chopped coriander/cilantro. Stir in the squeezed courgette/zucchini and corn kernels, ensuring the vegetables are evenly coated in batter.

★ Add enough sunflower oil to thinly cover the bottom of a heavy-bottomed frying pan/skillet. Drop small spoonfuls of batter into the pan using a teaspoon and cook for about 2 minutes on each side, until golden brown. Drain on paper towels, then transfer to a clean baking sheet. Cook the remaining batter in the same way, adding a little more oil to the pan each time, if required. If you are not going to assemble the blinis straight away, cool completely and cover with clingfilm/plastic wrap.

★ To make the Lemon Cream, combine the sour cream, lemon juice and zest and salt in a small bowl.

★ Arrange the blinis on a serving platter, top with a ribbon of smoked salmon and a dollop of Lemon Cream. Garnish with chervil or chopped chives and a sprinkle of freshly ground black pepper.

GRILLED HALLOUMI
with blistered jalapeño, lime & tequila relish

- -

SALTY HALLOUMI CHEESE WORKS VERY WELL ALONGSIDE STRONG FLAVOURS, SUCH AS THOSE IN THIS DIVINE, TANGY RELISH, WHICH YOU WILL SOON BE DOLLOPING ON EVERYTHING. WHY NOT KEEP TO THE TEQUILA THEME AND SERVE THESE WITH COOLING ICED MARGARITAS?

450 g/1 lb. halloumi

3 tablespoons olive oil

grated zest and juice of 2 limes

cracked black pepper, for sprinkling

extra limes, for squeezing

serves 6

for the blistered jalapeño, lime & tequila relish

3 tablespoons olive oil, plus extra for oiling

4 jalapeño chillies/chiles or other type of fresh chilli/chile

1 red and 1 white onion, thinly sliced

3 garlic cloves, finely chopped

grated zest of 1 lime

2 tablespoons tequila

3 tablespoons clear honey

60 ml/¼ cup white wine vinegar

sea salt

still-warm sterilized glass jars with airtight lids

makes 475 ml/2 cups

★ For the relish, put a lightly-oiled large frying pan/skillet over a high heat until smoking. Add the jalapeños, lower the heat slightly and cook until the skins are charred and blistered. Remove from the pan and set aside to cool.

★ Add the oil, sliced onions and garlic to the pan and cook over a medium heat for 5 minutes, stirring occasionally. Season with salt to taste. Add the lime zest with the onion.

★ Roughly chop the cooled jalapeños and add to the pan along with the tequila, honey and vinegar. Cook for a further 10 minutes, until the onions are golden brown and soft.

★ Pack the relish into warm sterilized glass jars, leaving a 5-mm/¼-inch space at the top, and carefully tap the jars on the counter to get rid of any air pockets. Wipe the jars clean and screw on the lids. Seal the jars for 15 minutes in a preheated oven at 120°C (250°F) or for 10 minutes using a water bath set to the same temperature. Once sealed, store unopened in a cool, dark place for up to 12 months.

★ Slice the halloumi into 5-mm/¼-inch pieces. Put a heavy-bottom frying pan/skillet over a medium–high heat and pour in the olive oil. Swirl the pan to coat. Working in batches, add the halloumi and sauté on each side for 2 minutes. Add a little lime zest and juice to the pan per batch. The halloumi will cook quickly, so keep an eye on it.

★ Transfer the cheese to a warm serving platter.

★ Put a teaspoon of relish on top of each piece of cheese. Sprinkle with cracked black pepper and finish with an extra squeeze of lime. Serve immediately.

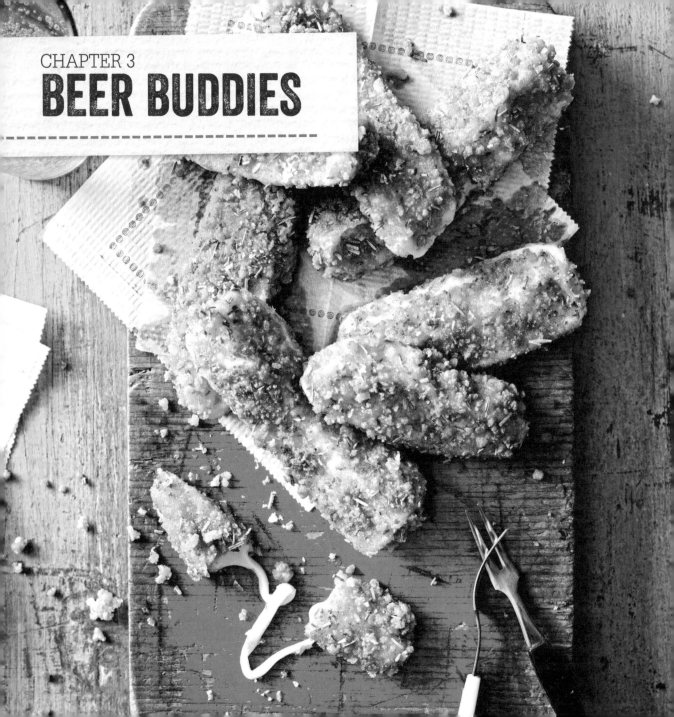

DEEP-FRIED MOZZARELLA CHEESE STICKS

WARM, CRISPY, GOOEY CHEESE STICKS ARE A GREAT ANTIDOTE TO THOSE PARTICULAR MUNCHIES YOU GET AFTER A COUPLE OF BEERS. THESE ARE SO EASY TO MAKE AND YOUR GUESTS WILL LOVE YOU FOR IT! SERVE WITH PLENTY OF CONDIMENTS FOR DUNKING.

2 eggs, beaten

120 g/1½ cups Italian-seasoned breadcrumbs

½ teaspoon garlic salt

80 g/⅔ cup plain/all-purpose flour

40 g/⅓ cup cornflour/cornstarch

450-g/1-lb. bag of mozzarella cheese sticks

vegetable oil, for frying

an electric deep fryer

serves 4–6

★ In a small bowl, mix the beaten eggs with 60 ml/¼ cup water.

★ In a separate, medium bowl, mix the breadcrumbs and garlic salt together. In another medium bowl, mix the flour and cornflour/cornstarch together.

★ Preheat the oil in a deep fryer set to 180°C (350°F).

★ One at a time, coat each mozzarella stick in flour, then egg and then breadcrumbs. Fry for about 30 seconds until golden brown. Drain on paper towels before serving.

BEER-BATTERED ONION RINGS

375 g/3 cups plain/all-purpose flour

2 eggs, separated

250 ml/1 cup beer (such as IPA, Pilsner or German lager)

60 g/4 tablespoons butter, melted and cooled

sea salt and freshly ground black pepper

3 large yellow or white onions, sliced into rings

vegetable oil, for frying

an *electric deep fryer*

serves 4–6

SOMETIMES THERE IS SIMPLY NOTHING BETTER THAN A CRISPY, BEER-BATTERED ONION RING. THEY ARE AN IDEAL BAR SNACK TO GORGE ON AND GO VERY WELL WITH THE DEEP-FRIED MOZZARELLA CHEESE STICKS (SEE PAGE 39), IF YOU'RE FEELING DECADENT.

★ Sift the flour into a large bowl. Set aside one-third of the flour for dredging the onions.

★ In a separate, large bowl, whisk the egg yolks. Mix in the beer, melted butter and salt and pepper. Slowly stir the egg yolk and beer mixture into the bowl containing two-thirds of the flour and mix well. Allow the mixture to stand for 30–60 minutes.

★ Preheat the oil in a deep fryer set to 180°C (350°F).

★ In a small bowl, beat the egg whites until stiff peaks are formed. Fold the egg whites into the batter.

★ Coat each onion ring with flour, then dip into the batter. Fry several at a time, until golden brown. Serve immediately.

FRIED GREEN TOMATOES

FRIED GREEN TOMATOES ARE POPULAR IN THE SOUTHERN PART OF THE US. THIS RECIPE IS SIMPLE TO PREPARE – FRYING UNRIPENED TOMATOES IN VEGETABLE OIL AFTER COATING THEM WITH A MIXTURE OF FLOUR, POLENTA AND A LITTLE SALT AND PEPPER. PANKO BREADCRUMBS ARE IDEAL FOR THIS RECIPE AND ARE AVAILABLE FROM LARGE SUPERMARKETS OR ASIAN FOOD STORES.

★ Chop the tomatoes into 1-cm/½-inch thick slices, discarding the ends. You should have 4–5 pieces per tomato. Set aside on a large plate.

★ In a medium bowl, whisk the eggs and milk together.

★ Measure out the flour and put it on a plate. In a separate bowl, whisk together the polenta/cornmeal, breadcrumbs, salt and pepper and transfer the mixture to a plate.

★ First, dip the tomato slices into the flour to coat, then dip them into the milk and egg mixture. Finally, dip them into the breadcrumb mixture so that they are completely covered in them.

★ Pour vegetable oil to a depth of 1 cm/½ inch into a large frying pan/skillet and heat over a medium heat. When the oil is steadily bubbling, carefully place the tomatoes into the frying pan/skillet in batches of 4–5, depending on the size of your frying pan/skillet. Do not crowd the tomatoes – they should not touch each other. When the tomatoes are browned, flip and fry them on the other side. Alternatively, use a deep fryer set to 180°C (350°F). Drain the fried tomatoes on paper towels and serve immediately.

4 large green tomatoes

2 eggs

125 ml/½ cup milk

120 g/1 cup plain/all-purpose flour

65 g/½ cup polenta/fine cornmeal

60 g/½ cup panko or ordinary breadcrumbs

2 teaspoons coarse sea salt

¼ teaspoon freshly ground black pepper

vegetable oil, for frying

serves 4

JALAPEÑO POPPERS

JALAPEÑOS ARE PERFECT FOR THIS RECIPE. THEY HAVE A JUICY FLESH THAT TASTES DELICIOUS WHEN COMBINED WITH A STRONG CHEESE SUCH AS MATURE/SHARP CHEDDAR. IF JALAPEÑOS ARE NOT AVAILABLE, USE RED CHERRY BOMB CHILLIES/CHILES WHICH ARE A LITTLE SWEETER AND OFTEN A LITTLE HOTTER TOO. THESE POPPERS MAKE FOR MOUTHWATERING BITES TO SERVE WITH MEXICAN BEER.

20 jalapeño chillies/chiles

140 g/1¼ cups grated/shredded mature/sharp Cheddar

50 g/⅓ cup plain/all-purpose flour

1 egg, beaten

sunflower oil, for deep frying

cooking thermometer (optional)

makes 20

★ Slit the jalapeños along one side and carefully remove the seeds. Stuff them generously with the grated/shredded Cheddar.

★ Put the flour in one shallow bowl and the beaten egg in another. Roll the jalapeños in the flour, dip in the egg and then coat once more with flour, ensuring that they are completely covered.

★ Half-fill a large saucepan with oil. Heat until the oil reaches 190°C (375°F) on a cooking thermometer. If you don't have a cooking thermometer, the oil is ready when a 2.5-cm/1-inch cube of white bread dropped into it browns in less than 60 seconds. Alternatively, use a deep fryer set to 180°C (350°F).

★ Fry the jalapeños in small batches for 6–7 minutes until golden. Remove with a slotted spoon and drain on paper towels. Serve immediately.

150 g/1 cup polenta/fine cornmeal

2 tablespoons plain/all-purpose flour

¼ teaspoon bicarbonate of soda/baking soda

3 teaspoons baking powder

½ teaspoon rock salt flakes

½ teaspoon ground white pepper

180 ml/¾ cup buttermilk

1 egg, lightly beaten

225 g/8 oz. raw prawns/shrimp, deveined

140 g/1 cup fresh corn kernels

2 spring onions/scallions, sliced

1 jalapeño, finely chopped

vegetable oil, for deep frying

coarse sea salt, to serve

makes approximately 20

for the corn & poblano relish

3 poblano chillies/chiles

2 tablespoons olive oil

2 garlic cloves, finely chopped

1 red onion, finely diced

1 red/bell pepper, finely diced

420 g/3 cups corn kernels

6 spring onions/scallions, sliced

grated zest and freshly squeezed juice of 1 lime

1 tablespoon Aleppo pepper flakes

150 g/¾ cup light brown sugar

425 ml/1¾ cups cider vinegar

makes 950 ml/4 cups

SOUTHERN SHRIMP HUSHPUPPIES with corn & poblano relish

THESE ICONIC SOUTHERN SAVOURY BITES ARE NAMED AFTER THE TITBITS HUNTERS CARRIED TO HUSH THEIR DOGS WHILE STALKING PREY. THIS MODERN VERSION IS MUCH MORE GLAMOROUS, THOUGH!

★ First, make the relish. Put a lightly-oiled large frying pan/skillet over a high heat until smoking. Add the chillies/chiles, lower the heat slightly and cook until the skins are charred and blistered. Remove and set aside to cool.

★ Once cool, roughly chop the chillies/chiles and set aside. Return the pan to a medium heat and add the olive oil, garlic, red onion and bell pepper, and sauté for 5 minutes. Add the chopped poblanos, corn kernels, spring onions/scallions, lime zest and juice, and Aleppo pepper, and stir. Add the sugar, pour in the vinegar and season with salt and pepper. Stir and bring to a boil, then reduce the heat and simmer for 15–20 minutes.

★ Put the polenta/cornmeal, flour, bicarbonate of soda/baking soda, baking powder, salt and pepper in a large bowl and mix together. Pour in the buttermilk and egg and mix together. Add the prawns/shrimp, corn kernels, onions and jalapeño and mix well to combine.

★ Put a deep frying pan/skillet over a medium–high heat and add enough oil to come three-quarters of the way up the pan. Heat the oil to 180°C (350°F). Using a small ice cream scoop, and working in batches, drop the hushpuppies into the hot fat. Sauté for 5 minutes or until golden. Transfer to a warm serving plate. Sprinkle with coarse sea salt and serve with the relish.

GARLIC & HERB DOUGH BALLS

ENJOY THESE MOREISH SAVOURY BREAD ROLLS FRESHLY BAKED AND WARM FROM THE OVEN. MAKE SURE YOU HAVE ENOUGH GARLIC AND HERB BUTTER LEFT OVER AT THE END SO YOU CAN BRUSH OR DRIZZLE IT OVER. A GREAT GRAB-AND-GO ITALIAN-STYLE SNACK.

500 g/3½ cups strong/bread flour, plus extra for dusting

1 teaspoon fast-action dried yeast

1½ teaspoons sea salt

1½ teaspoons sugar

300 ml/1¼ cups hand-hot water

2 tablespoons olive oil, plus extra for greasing

75 g/⅓ cup butter, softened

4 garlic cloves, crushed

a small handful of fresh flat-leaf parsley, finely chopped

2 baking sheets, lightly greased

makes 24

★ First, make the bread dough. In a mixing bowl, mix together the flour, yeast, salt and sugar. Gradually add the hand-hot water and olive oil, bringing the mixture together to form a sticky dough. Turn out onto a lightly floured surface and knead well until the dough is smooth and elastic. Place in a clean, oiled mixing bowl, cover with a damp, clean tea/dish towel and set aside in a warm place to prove for 1 hour, during which time it should rise noticeably and almost double in size.

★ While the dough is rising, mix the softened butter, garlic and parsley together thoroughly.

★ Preheat the oven to 220°C (425°F) Gas 7.

★ Gently heat the garlic and herb butter in a pan until just melted.

★ Knock back the risen dough and divide it into 24 even-sized portions, shaping each into a rounded ball shape. Put the dough balls on the greased baking sheets, spaced well apart. Brush each dough ball generously with the melted garlic and herb butter.

★ Bake the dough balls for 15–20 minutes in the preheated oven until golden brown. Brush the freshly baked dough balls with the remaining butter and serve immediately.

FRENCH FRIES

1.1 kg/2½ lbs. russet or baking potatoes, peeled

130 g/1 cup plain/all-purpose flour

1 teaspoon garlic salt

1 teaspoon onion salt

1 teaspoon sea salt

1 teaspoon smoked paprika

1 teaspoon cayenne pepper or other seasoning of your choice (optional)

125 ml/½ cup beer or water, or more as needed

vegetable oil, for frying

an electric deep fryer

serves 4–6

THE CLASSIC FEEL-GOOD BAR BITE, THESE ARE PERFECT ON THEIR OWN OR AS PART OF A LARGER SELECTION OF SNACKS. THE ONION AND GARLIC SALT GIVES THEM A LOVELY SAVOURY FLAVOUR WHILE THE PAPRIKA ADDS A NICE SMOKINESS. ENJOY THEM PLAIN OR DUNK THEM IN YOUR CHOICE OF SAUCE.

★ Carefully slice the potatoes into French fries and place into a big bowl of cold water (this prevents them turning brown while the oil is heating).

★ Preheat the oil in a deep fryer set to 180°C (350°F).

★ While the oil is heating, mix the flour, garlic salt, onion salt, regular salt and smoked paprika and extra seasoning of your choice in a large bowl with a whisk. Gradually stir in enough beer or water so that the mixture can be drizzled from a spoon.

★ Dip the fries in the batter one at a time, and carefully lower into the hot oil so they are not touching at first (the fries need to be placed into the fryer one at a time, or they will clump together). Fry until golden brown and crispy. Remove and drain on paper towels. Serve with a dipping sauce of your choice.

SWEET POTATO FRIES

4 sweet potatoes, cut to desired size and thickness

2–3 tablespoons olive oil

1 tablespoon sea salt

1 tablespoon freshly ground black pepper

¼ teaspoon cayenne pepper (optional)

2 large baking sheets, greased liberally with olive oil

serves 4

IF YOU'RE CRAVING A HIGH-FAT AND SALTY TREAT LIKE FRENCH FRIES, TRY THIS DELICIOUS BAKED ALTERNATIVE INSTEAD. THE CRISP, CARAMELIZED EDGE CONCEALS A SOFT AND SWEET CENTRE. THIS RECIPE CALLS FOR OLIVE OIL, BUT COCONUT OIL CAN BE USED INSTEAD IF YOU LIKE.

★ Preheat the oven to 200°C (400°F) Gas 6.

★ In a resealable plastic bag, combine the sweet potatoes, olive oil, salt, pepper and cayenne pepper (if using). Close and shake the bag until the sweet potatoes are evenly coated. Spread them out in a single layer on the baking sheets.

★ Bake in the preheated oven for 20 minutes, or until the sweet potatoes are crispy and brown on one side. Turn the fries over using a spatula, and cook for another 15–20 minutes, or until they are all crispy on the outside and tender inside.

SMOKED CHIPOTLE WINGS

3 large handfuls of hickory wood chips, divided

1.8 kg/4 lbs. chicken wings, halved at the joints, tips removed

6 tablespoons Cajun seasoning, or as needed

3 tablespoons butter

3 tablespoons finely chopped garlic

1 litre/4 cups hot sauce (such as Frank's Red Hot®)

vegetable oil, for frying

lime wedges, to serve

for the chipotle-sour cream dip

210-g/7-oz. can of chipotle chillies/chiles in adobo sauce

450 ml/2 cups sour cream

1 tablespoon ground cumin

freshly squeezed juice of 1 lime

sea salt

a smoker

an electric deep fryer

serves 4–6

EVERYONE LOVES TO DIG INTO A BIG SHARING PLATTER OF CHICKEN WINGS, AND THIS IS THE ULTIMATE RECIPE! IT USES A SMOKER WITH HICKORY WOOD CHIPS TO CREATE A RICH FLAVOUR. THE WINGS ARE THEN FRIED AND GRILLED, GIVING THEM A BEAUTIFUL CRISPY TEXTURE.

★ Preheat the smoker to 95°C (200°F) and add 1 handful of wood chips to start the smoke rolling.

★ Liberally coat the chicken wings with half of the Cajun seasoning.

★ Place the wings directly on the grate in the smoker or in an aluminium pan with holes to allow airflow. Smoke the wings for 2 hours, adding more wood chips as necessary.

★ Meanwhile, make the dip. Put the chillies/chiles in a blender with the sour cream, cumin, lime juice and a few good pinches of salt. Pulse in the blender until well combined. Refrigerate for at least 2 hours before serving.

★ Combine the butter, garlic and remaining Cajun seasoning in a large saucepan over a medium heat. Cook the mixture for about 1 minute, stirring, until the butter has melted. Stir the hot sauce into the butter mixture and lower the heat, simmering the mixture for about 30 minutes, stirring occasionally, until the sauce has thickened.

★ Preheat the oil in a deep fryer set to 190°C (375°F). Preheat a grill/broiler to medium–hot.

★ Remove the wings from the smoker and cook, 10–12 at a time, in the deep fryer for 5–7 minutes, until they are cooked through and are lightly browned on the outside.

★ Transfer the cooked wings to a baking sheet and liberally coat each wing with hot sauce mixture. Put the coated wings directly onto the wire rack of the preheated grill/broiler and cook for 2–3 minutes on each side, until the sauce has caramelized and the wings are crisp. Serve with the dip and with wedges of lime.

SPICED FRIED CHICKEN

3 skinless chicken breasts

150 ml/⅔ cup buttermilk

100 g/¾ cup plain/all-purpose flour

1 generous teaspoon baking powder

1 generous teaspoon sea salt flakes

½ teaspoon ground cayenne pepper

½ teaspoon smoked paprika

¼ teaspoon ground coriander

¼ teaspoon garlic powder

a pinch of ground allspice

½ teaspoon dried oregano

freshly ground black pepper

sunflower oil, for frying

serves 4

MARINATING CHICKEN IN BUTTERMILK TENDERIZES THE MEAT AND MAKES THESE LITTLE BITES REALLY JUICY. SERVE WITH PLENTY OF SPICY MAYO FOR DIPPING. THEY ARE SO MUCH NICER THAN THE TAKEAWAY NUGGET VERSION, JUST TRY THEM YOURSELF AND SEE!

★ Cut each chicken breast into 5 or 6 strips. Place in a ceramic dish and coat with the buttermilk. Cover with clingfilm/plastic wrap and chill for at least 2 hours.

★ Remove the chicken from the buttermilk and pat off any excess with paper towels. Combine the flour, baking powder, salt flakes, spices, oregano and some black pepper in a bowl. Toss the chicken pieces in the seasoned flour and set aside on baking parchment for 10 minutes.

★ Pour 3–4 tablespoons sunflower oil in a frying pan/skillet. Set over a medium heat and add one-third of the chicken pieces. Cook until golden and crispy.

★ Drain on paper towels and repeat with the remaining batches of chicken.

SOLE GOUJONS

A FANCY BITE-SIZE VERSION OF FISH AND CHIPS, THIS RECIPE INVOLVES FRYING THE BREADCRUMBS UNTIL GOLDEN IN A LITTLE OLIVE OIL AND BUTTER – THIS WAY THE FISH CAN BE BAKED IN THE OVEN RATHER THAN DEEP-FRIED. SERVE THE GOUJONS ON A SHARING PLATTER WITH KETCHUP, TARTARE SAUCE AND FRENCH FRIES.

2 tablespoons olive oil

2 tablespoons unsalted butter

200 g/4 cups fresh, fine breadcrumbs

1 tablespoon freshly chopped flat-leaf parsley

2 teaspoons freshly chopped thyme

finely grated zest of 1 unwaxed lemon

1 teaspoon smoked paprika

450 g/1 lb. skinless sole fillets

4 tablespoons plain/all-purpose flour

2 eggs, beaten

sea salt and freshly ground black pepper

to serve

French Fries (see page 46)

tomato ketchup

tartare sauce

lemon wedges

a baking sheet, lined with baking parchment

serves 4

★ Preheat the oven to 220°C (425°F) Gas 7.

★ Heat the oil and butter in a large frying pan/skillet, add the breadcrumbs and, stirring constantly, cook until golden. Tip the crumbs into a large bowl, add the chopped herbs, lemon zest and smoked paprika and season well with salt and black pepper. Leave to cool.

★ Cut each sole fillet into strips roughly 3-cm/1-inch wide.

★ Tip the flour into one shallow dish and the beaten eggs into another. Taking one piece of fish at a time, coat it first in the flour, then the beaten eggs, then the golden breadcrumbs. Arrange the goujons on the prepared baking sheet and bake in the preheated oven for about 10 minutes, or until cooked through.

★ Serve immediately with French Fries, tomato ketchup, tartare sauce and lemon wedges.

VIETNAMESE CHICKEN PIES

AN INTERESTING TAKE ON THE CLASSIC PIE. THE FRENCH LEFT A DISTINCTIVE MARK ON VIETNAMESE CUISINE AND THIS LIGHT PUFFY SNACK IS ONE STREET-FOOD EXAMPLE. THE VIETNAMESE ENJOY PASTRY SNACKS LIKE THESE OFTEN. THEY ARE ESPECIALLY EASY TO MAKE WITH READY-ROLLED FROZEN PUFF PASTRY. THEY CAN ALSO BE FILLED WITH CHICKEN CURRY OR BEEF STEW FOR A DELICIOUS ALTERNATIVE.

100 g/3½ oz. skinless chicken breast

1 teaspoon cooking oil

2 tablespoons butter

3 garlic cloves, finely chopped

2 chestnut mushrooms, finely chopped

50 g/⅓ cup garden peas

1 teaspoon pork stock/bouillon

1 teaspoon sugar

½ teaspoon freshly ground black pepper

1 tablespoon tapioca starch

320 g/11 oz. ready-rolled puff pastry dough, thawed if frozen

1 egg yolk, lightly beaten

chilli/chile sauce, such as Sriracha, to serve

a 6-cm/2½-inch round cookie cutter or glass

a baking sheet, greased

makes 6

★ Chop the chicken into 1-cm/½-inch cubes or quickly pulse into pieces in a food processor.

★ Heat the oil in a saucepan over a medium heat, then add the chicken, butter, garlic, mushrooms, peas, pork stock/bouillon, sugar and pepper. Fry until the chicken is golden.

★ Put the tapioca starch and 5 tablespoons water in a bowl and stir together. Pour into the pan and stir well. This will thicken and bind everything together. Cook for 1 minute, then remove from the heat and allow to rest while you prepare the pastry.

★ Preheat the oven to 180°C (350°F) Gas 4.

★ Unroll the puff pastry dough on a lightly floured surface. Use the cookie cutter or upturned glass to stamp out 12 rounds from the dough. Brush egg yolk over all the rounds with a pastry brush. Put each pastry round on your hand and put a generous tablespoon of fried, cooled filling in the centre. Place on the prepared baking sheet, top with the remaining rounds and press the tines of a fork all around the edges to seal the 2 pastry rounds together.

★ Bake the pies in the preheated oven for about 35 minutes or until golden. Serve immediately, with chilli/chile sauce for dipping.

MICHAELMAS PIE

250 g/9 oz. game, such as venison, rabbit and pheasant, diced (alternatively, diced beef is delicious in this pie too)

2 tablespoons butter

½ garlic clove, chopped

100 g/1½ cups chopped mushrooms

40 g/generous ¼ cup plain/all-purpose flour

20 g/4 teaspoons tomato purée/paste

100 ml/scant ½ cup red wine

80 ml/⅓ cup beef stock/bouillon

40 g/2 tablespoons redcurrant jelly

a sprig of fresh thyme

2 bay leaves

sea salt and freshly ground black pepper, to season

1 beaten egg or 20 ml/4 teaspoons milk, to glaze

for the pastry

100 g/7 tablespoons salted butter

225 g/1¾ cups plain/all-purpose flour

a pinch of sea salt

3–4 tablespoons chilled water

8 individual round pie dishes, greased

makes 8 mini pies

THE FILLING IS SUCH A SIMPLE THROW-TOGETHER RECIPE, BUT IT TASTES TERRIFIC WITH THE SWEETNESS OF THE REDCURRANT JELLY.

★ Start by making the pastry. Rub the butter, flour and a little salt together with your fingertips until the mixture resembles breadcrumbs. Then keep adding a little chilled water, a tablespoonful at a time, until you can combine the crumbled mixture into a ball of pastry. Don't add too much water. Wrap in clingfilm/plastic wrap and chill while you make the pie filling.

★ Preheat the oven to 180°C (350°F) Gas 4.

★ Put the diced game, butter, garlic, mushrooms, flour, tomato purée/paste, red wine, stock, redcurrant jelly, thyme, bay leaves and some seasoning into a stewing pot (or a pan with a lid) stir, cover with the lid and cook in the preheated oven for 90 minutes. Every 20 minutes or so, take it out and give it a stir; everything will cook really easily and the mixture will start to thicken. Just make sure the flour hasn't stuck to the side or formed an unintentional dumpling – if it has, break it up with a spoon.

★ On a floured work surface, roll the pastry to a thickness of 5-mm/¼-inch using a floured rolling pin. Cut out 8 circles and place them into your pie dishes. Make sure there's enough pastry left over to make the lids.

★ Remove the filling from the oven, but leave the oven on. Remove the sprig of thyme and bay leaves from the mixture and divide the filling between the pastry-lined pie dishes.

★ Use the rest of the pastry to make the lids. Place them on top of the pies, using beaten egg or milk to stick the edges to the lids, crimping the pastry with your fingers.

★ Brush the remaining egg or milk over the top and use a sharp knife to make one or two little holes in the middle of the lids.

★ Cook the pies in the oven for 25 minutes until the pastry is cooked and browning.

SCOTCH QUAILS' EGGS

BITE-SIZE EGGS ARE SO MUCH MORE FUN THAN THE FULL SIZE VARIETY AND QUAILS' EGGS ARE PACKED WITH PROTEIN. A NICE WAY TO SERVE THEM IS TO MIX A LITTLE MUSTARD WITH MAYONNAISE AND SERVE ON THE SIDE AS A DIP.

12 quails' eggs

600 g/20 oz. good-quality pork sausages

1 tablespoon finely chopped fresh flat-leaf parsley

1 tablespoon finely chopped fresh thyme (optional)

1 egg yolk, beaten, plus 1 whole egg

1 tablespoon plain/all-purpose flour

4 tablespoons milk

75 g/1 cup fine breadcrumbs

sunflower oil, for frying

sea salt and freshly ground black pepper, to season

makes 12

★ Bring a small saucepan of water to a boil and gently lower in the quails' eggs. Boil for 100 seconds, then plunge the boiled eggs immediately into cold water to stop further cooking. Once cold, one at a time, roll each egg gently along a work surface with the flat of your palm until the shell is all crackled, then peel away the shell. Set the peeled eggs aside until needed.

★ Remove the skins from the sausages and discard and put the sausage meat in a large mixing bowl with the parsley, thyme, if using, and egg yolk. Season with salt and pepper and stir to combine. Divide the mixture into 12 equal portions.

★ Now get three shallow bowls ready, the first holding the plain/all-purpose flour seasoned with salt and pepper, the next with a whole egg beaten with the milk, and the last bowl filled with the breadcrumbs.

★ Take a portion of sausage meat and make a patty with it in your palm. Place a quail's egg in the centre and gently mould the sausage meat around it before rolling it into a ball between your palms. Repeat with the rest of the sausage meat and quails' eggs. Roll each scotch egg firstly in seasoned flour, then dip it in the egg wash before coating it in the breadcrumbs.

★ Pour the oil into a saucepan and bring up to smoking hot temperature, (around 180°C/350°F). Alternatively, use an electric deep fryer. Fry a few eggs at a time for about 4 minutes until they are golden brown all over. Transfer to a plate lined with paper towels to soak up any excess oil and leave to cool before serving.

ULTIMATE GRILLED CHEESE SANDWICH

THERE'S PROBABLY NO BETTER COMFORT FOOD THAN THE GRILLED CHEESE SANDWICH. IT IS FANTASTICALLY VERSATILE, AS IT CAN BE AS SIMPLE OR AS PIMPED UP AS YOU LIKE. THIS RECIPE IS A MAJOR UPGRADE FROM A BASIC GRILLED CHEESE AND WON'T DISAPPOINT AS A TEMPTING BUT UNFUSSY BAR SNACK THAT WILL SATISFY NICELY.

for the cured tomatoes

1–2 tomatoes

200 ml/1 scant cup olive oil

60 g/1 cup homemade breadcrumbs, toasted

a pinch of sea salt

to assemble the sandwiches

12 slices bacon

12 slices sourdough bread, cut 1-cm/½-inch thick

6 tablespoons salted butter, at room temperature

4 tablespoons Dijonnaise, made by mixing mayonnaise and a little Dijon mustard

25 g/¼ cup freshly grated Parmesan

115 g/4 oz. mature/sharp Cheddar, grated

115 g/4 oz. Gouda, grated

115 g/4 oz. Provolone, grated

1½ teaspoons sea salt

½ teaspoon freshly ground black pepper

an oven-safe frying pan/skillet

makes 6

★ Slice the tomatoes to a thickness of 1 cm/½ inch. Lay them in a pie dish and add olive oil until the slices are half-submerged. Let the tomatoes sit for 30 minutes, turning once. After that time, lift the tomatoes out of the oil and season them with salt. Press them into the homemade toasted breadcrumbs.

★ Preheat oven to 160°C (325°F) Gas 3.

★ Fry the bacon until nicely browned. Drain the slices on paper towels, cool and cut into 2.5 cm/1-inch pieces.

★ Lay the slices of bread on a bread board and spread each one lightly with butter. Flip the slices and spread generously with Dijonnaise. Layer the bacon over the top and add a couple of slices of the cured tomatoes.

★ Mix the cheeses together in a bowl. Pile a handful of the mixed cheeses on top of the bacon on each sandwich. Top with the remaining bread slices, mayonnaise side down.

★ Put the sandwiches in an oven-safe frying pan/skillet in a preheated oven for a few minutes so the cheese melts nicely. Remove the sandwiches from the oven and leave to cool for 2 minutes before serving.

CRISPY PORK BELLY BITES

85 g/¼ cup clear honey

5 bay leaves

3 fresh rosemary sprigs

250 g/1 cup sea salt

2 tablespoons peppercorns

a small bunch of fresh thyme

1 garlic bulb, cloves removed and flattened with skin on

1.5 kg/4½ lbs. pork belly, skin on

2 litres/8 cups olive oil

fresh coriander/cilantro, roughly chopped, to garnish

a baking sheet, greased and lined with baking parchment

serves 8–10

DON'T BE PUT OFF BY THE STEPS AS THESE PERFECT PARTY BITES ARE NOT DIFFICULT. THEY CAN BE PREPARED DAYS IN ADVANCE AND THEN GRILLED/BROILED IN MINUTES WHEN READY TO SERVE.

★ Begin by brining the pork. Combine the honey, bay leaves, rosemary, salt, peppercorns, thyme, garlic and 3 litres/12 cups of water in a container large enough to hold the pork. Place the pork in the brine, cover and set in the fridge for at least 12 hours or overnight.

★ Remove the pork from the brine and discard the brine. Rinse the pork in a large bowl under running water, then pat dry with paper towels.

★ To confit the pork, preheat the oven to 120°C (250°F) Gas ½. Put the rinsed pork in a roasting pan and pour over the olive oil. Cover with foil and cook in the preheated oven for 4½ hours. The oil will gently bubble and poach the pork, until it is soft and falling apart.

★ Remove the pork from the oven, uncover slightly and allow it to cool to room temperature.

★ Press the pork so that it has a nice, firm texture, by removing it from the oil and place it, rind-side down, on the prepared baking sheet. Keep the oil to one side for crisping the skin later. Cover the pork with clingfilm/plastic wrap and weigh it down with something heavy like a big wooden chopping board or a cast-iron roasting dish. Set in the fridge for at least 12 hours.

★ When ready to serve, preheat the oven to 220°C (425°F) Gas 7.

★ Score the skin of the pressed pork with a diamond pattern and cut into 2-cm/¾-inch squares.

★ Drizzle a clean baking sheet with a little of the reserved cooking oil, place the pork squares skin-side down and roast for 15 minutes, until the skin is golden brown and crisp. Remove from the oven and drain on paper towels. Alternatively, you can crisp up the skin by placing the pork, skin-side up, underneath a grill/broiler on a medium heat for 3–4 minutes.

★ Transfer to a serving platter, garnish with coriander/cilantro and serve with your choice of dipping sauce on the side.

PORK RILLETTES

RILLETTES ARE LIKE A PÂTÉ WITH A BIT MORE TEXTURE, BECAUSE THE MEAT IS SHREDDED, RATHER THAN PURÉED. THEY ARE BEST SERVED AT ROOM TEMPERATURE, WITH SOME MELBA TOAST OR CRISPBREAD.

200 g/7 oz. pork belly (rindless), trimmed and diced

1 tablespoon sea salt

2 tablespoons butter

1 garlic clove, finely chopped

a small pinch of ground mace

1 bay leaf

a pinch of freshly chopped or dried parsley

50 ml/scant ¼ cup dry white wine

150 ml/⅔ cup chicken stock

sea salt and freshly ground black pepper

freshly squeezed lemon juice and freshly chopped parsley, to serve (optional)

melba toast, to serve

gherkins, to serve

serves 2

★ Put the pork belly in a non-metallic container and sprinkle the salt over the top. Massage the salt into the meat, then cover tightly and refrigerate for 1–2 hours. Rinse and dry the pork cubes – the salt should have already drawn some of the moisture out of the pork belly, but you don't want to draw out too much because you're going to slow-cook it, which will benefit from keeping the fat.

★ Melt the butter in a saucepan over a medium heat (you're going to need a saucepan with a lid), then add the pork belly, garlic, mace, bay leaf and parsley, and season with salt and pepper. Cook, stirring often, to slightly brown the pork and coat it in the seasoning, then add the white wine and increase the heat to high for 1–2 minutes to reduce the wine. Pour in the chicken stock.

★ Turn the heat down to very low and put the lid on the pan. Leave it cooking gently for 1¼ hours. At this stage, press one of the cubes of pork with a fork and if it starts to fall apart, it's had long enough. However, it's likely that it'll need a little longer. If the mixture is starting to dry out and stick to the bottom of the pan, just add another splash of chicken stock – about 50 ml/ scant ¼ cup. Replace the lid and leave to cook gently for another 20–30 minutes, until the meat is falling apart. Remove from the heat and leave to cool. Discard the bay leaf.

★ The best way to shred the pork is with your fingers, so let it cool enough to touch, then pull it apart with your fingers and mix it well.

★ Transfer the pork to a container or 2 ramekins and chill in the fridge for at least 1 hour so that the mixture can set. It's worth bringing it out of the refrigerator about 30 minutes before serving – the texture of shredded meat is best at room temperature and it allows the flavour to come through really well. Feel free to add a squeeze of lemon juice before serving and a sprinkling of fresh parsley, if you like. Serve with melba toast and gherkins on the side.

250 g/2 sticks unsalted butter

3 shallots, sliced

2 fresh thyme sprigs

2 garlic cloves, crushed

fresh grating of nutmeg

4 tablespoons port or Madeira

1 tablespoon olive oil

500 g/1 lb. chicken livers, trimmed

sea salt and freshly ground black pepper

toasted brioche, to serve

for the fig relish

125 g/4 oz. ready-to-eat dried figs, roughly chopped

50 g/⅓ cup stoned/pitted dates, roughly chopped

1 shallot, sliced

1 small eating apple, peeled, cored and finely diced

2 tablespoons light muscovado sugar

125 ml/½ cup white wine vinegar or cider vinegar

1 teaspoon grated orange zest

1 cinnamon stick

1 fresh or dried bay leaf

a pâté terrine or serving dish

serves 4–6

CHICKEN LIVER PARFAIT
with fig relish & toasted brioche

THIS IS THE PERFECT SHARING DISH – JUST PUT THE TERRINE IN THE MIDDLE OF THE TABLE WITH A JAR OF THE RELISH, A STACK OF WARM TOASTED BRIOCHE, AND LET EVERYONE DIG IN.

★ Melt 2 tablespoons of the butter in a small saucepan, add the shallots and half the leaves from the thyme sprigs and cook over a low–medium heat until the shallots are soft but not coloured. Add the garlic and nutmeg and continue to cook for another minute. Add the port and cook until almost all the liquid has evaporated. Remove from the heat.

★ Heat the oil in a large frying pan/skillet and add half the chicken livers. Cook over a medium–high heat for a couple of minutes on each side until they are just cooked through but still pink in the middle. Tip the livers and the onion mixture into a food processor. Cook the remainder of the chicken livers in the same pan, then add to the food processor. Blend until smooth. Cut 175 g/1½ sticks of the butter into small pieces and gradually add to the mixture with the motor running. Push the mixture through a fine-mesh sieve/strainer into a bowl and season well with salt and black pepper.

★ Spoon the parfait into the terrine or serving dish and spread level. Melt the remaining butter, remove from the heat and leave for 2–3 minutes. Leave the cloudy whey on the bottom and spoon the melted butter from the top onto the parfait to cover it. Scatter the remaining thyme leaves over the top and allow to set and cool before chilling.

★ To make the relish, tip the ingredients into a saucepan. Cook over a low heat for 25 minutes or until tender. Remove the cinnamon and bay leaf, season and leave to cool before serving with the parfait and toasted brioche.

for the marinade

140 g/1 cup plain/all-purpose flour

½ teaspoon smoked paprika

½ teaspoon cayenne pepper

½ teaspoon sea salt

20 chicken wings

for the ranch dressing

250 ml/1 cup buttermilk, shaken

60 g/¼ cup mayonnaise

3 tablespoons sour cream

3 tablespoons fresh flat-leaf parsley, finely chopped

2 tablespoons fresh chives, finely chopped

4 teaspoons white wine vinegar or lemon juice

1 garlic clove, finely chopped

¼ teaspoon garlic powder

½ teaspoon sea salt, plus extra if needed

freshly ground black pepper

for the hot sauce

110 g/1 stick butter

125 ml/½ cup Louisiana hot sauce, or other hot sauce

2 pinches freshly ground black pepper

3 pinches garlic powder

vegetable oil, for frying

celery and carrots, for dipping

makes 20

BUFFALO CHICKEN WINGS
with homemade ranch dressing

TAKING THEIR NAME FROM THE CITY IN WHICH THEY ORIGINATED, BUFFALO, NEW YORK, BUFFALO WINGS HAVE BECOME AN AMERICAN STAPLE. THEY ARE OFTEN SERVED DURING SPORTING EVENTS OR AT LATE-NIGHT BARS TO A NO-DOUBT APPRECIATIVE CLIENTELE.

★ Combine the flour, smoked paprika, cayenne pepper and salt in a large resealable plastic bag. Shake the bag to combine the spices. Next, put the chicken wings in the bag, seal tightly and shake them to coat evenly in the spice mix. Place the bag in the fridge for 60–90 minutes.

★ Put all of the ranch dressing ingredients in a 500 ml/2 cup jar with a tight-fitting lid. Seal tightly and shake to evenly distribute all the ingredients. Taste and season with additional salt and pepper as desired. Refrigerate until chilled and the flavours have melded, about 1 hour. The dressing will last up to 3 days in the fridge.

★ Combine the butter, Louisiana or other hot pepper sauce and garlic powder in a small saucepan over a low heat. Warm until the butter is melted and the ingredients are well blended. Season with black pepper and set aside.

★ In a large, deep, frying pan/skillet, add the vegetable oil to a depth of 2.5–5 cm/1–2 inches and heat to 190°C (375°F) or until the oil is bubbling steadily. Alternatively, use an electric deep fryer and follow the instructions.

★ Put the wings into the heated oil and fry them for 10–15 minutes or until some parts of the wings begin to turn a golden to dark brown colour.

★ Remove the wings from the oil and drain on paper towels for a few seconds. Place the wings in a large bowl or in a large uncovered Tupperware box. Add the hot sauce mixture and stir, tossing the wings to thoroughly coat them.

★ Serve with the homemade Ranch Dressing and with a few sticks of celery and carrot on the side.

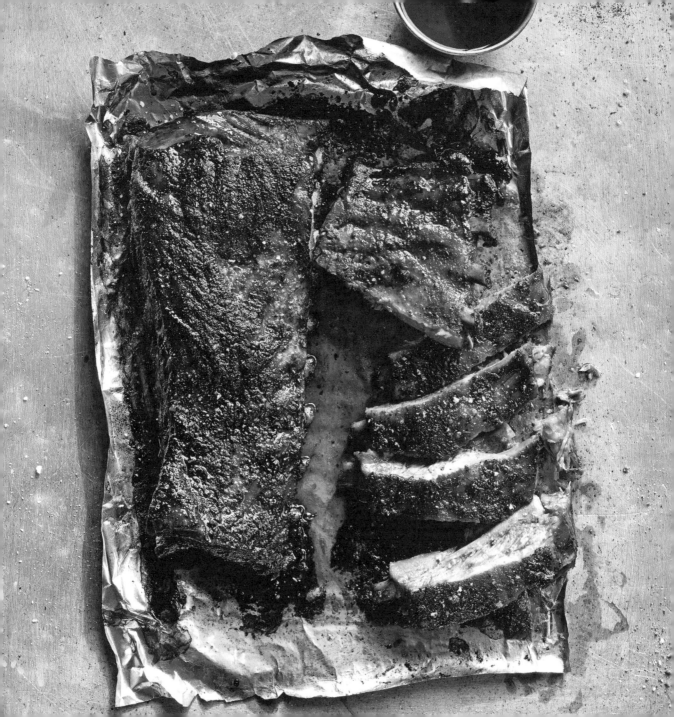

2 racks of baby back ribs

for the dry rub

1 tablespoon smoked paprika

1 teaspoon celery salt

1 teaspoon dark brown sugar

1 teaspoon garlic powder

¼ teaspoon mustard powder

¼ teaspoon dried thyme

¼ teaspoon ground white pepper

¼ teaspoon cayenne pepper

for the BBQ sauce

340 g/2½ cups tomato ketchup

115 g/½ cup golden syrup/molasses

125 ml/½ cup apple cider vinegar

1 teaspoon granulated sugar

½ teaspoon sea salt

½ teaspoon freshly ground black pepper

a charcoal grill or barbecue

serves 3–4

CHICAGO-STYLE BABY BACK RIBS

EVERYONE HAS THEIR OWN PREFERENCE WHEN IT COMES TO BBQ RIBS. SOME LIKE THEM RUBBED WITH SPICES WITH NO SAUCE, WHILE OTHERS SMOTHER SAUCE OVER THE TOP. CHICAGO-STYLE RIBS INVOLVE BOTH A RUB AND A SAUCE; FOR BEST RESULTS THEY'RE FIRST GRILLED SLOWLY THEN COOKED IN THE OVEN TO MAKE THEM REALLY TENDER.

★ Mix the dry rub ingredients together in a bowl. Rub the ribs with the spice mix and leave for 30 minutes.

★ Preheat a charcoal grill or barbecue. Cook the ribs over an indirect medium heat for 10–15 minutes.

★ Preheat the oven to 120°C (250°F) Gas ½.

★ Add about 1 cm/½ inch of water to an oblong baking sheet and place a grill rack into the pan. Place the ribs on the rack and cover tightly with foil. Bake for approximately 1½ hours and remove from the oven.

★ Mix all the sauce ingredients together with 125 ml/1½ cups water and spread over the ribs, reserving some to serve. Cover tightly again with foil and set aside for 15 minutes before serving. Serve along with the extra sauce for dipping.

2 tablespoons olive oil

½ medium white onion, finely diced

2 garlic cloves, finely chopped

1 jalapeño chilli/chile, finely diced

225 g/8 oz. minced/ground beef

2 teaspoons dried marjoram

2 teaspoons dried oregano

1 teaspoon sweet paprika

125 ml/½ cup red wine

2 quantities Pastry (see page 33)

1 egg, lightly beaten

sea salt and freshly ground black pepper

a 9-cm/3½-inch cookie cutter

a baking sheet lined with baking parchment

makes 28

for the Texan hot sauce

16 fresh red jalapeño chillies/chiles, stems removed

14 garlic cloves, peeled and bashed

3 tablespoons vegetable oil

1 tablespoon smoked paprika

2 tablespoons ancho chillies/chiles in adobo sauce

85 g/¼ cup honey

60 ml/¼ cup rice wine vinegar

55 g/¼ cup dark brown sugar

sterilized glass jars or bottles with airtight lids

makes 475 ml/2 cups

EMPANADAS with Texan hot sauce

THESE DELICIOUS LITTLE SPANISH PASTRY PARCELS FILLED WITH HERBED MEAT MAKE FOR FANTASTIC BAR SNACKS. BITE-SIZE AND DIPPED IN HOT SAUCE, THEY ARE HARD TO RESIST.

★ Preheat the oven to 190°C (375°F) Gas 5.

★ To make the hot sauce, put the jalapeños and garlic in a baking dish, drizzle with the oil and toss. Roast for 25–30 minutes, stirring halfway through. Remove from the oven and leave to cool before putting in a food processor. Add the sweet paprika, ancho chillies/chiles, honey, vinegar, sugar and a little water, then blend until smooth.

★ Pour the mixture into a non-reactive pan and bring to a boil. Reduce the heat and simmer for 15 minutes until the colour deepens. Pour into sterilized glass jars or bottles and carefully tap the jars on the counter to get rid of any air pockets. Wipe the jars clean and screw on the lids. Seal the jars for 15 minutes in a preheated oven at 120°C (250°F) Gas ½ or for 10 minutes using a water bath set to the same temperature. Once sealed, store unopened in a cool, dark place for up to 12 months.

★ Preheat the oven to 210°C (425°F) Gas 7.

★ Heat the olive oil in a frying pan/skillet over a medium–high heat, add the onion, garlic and jalapeños and cook for 5 minutes until golden brown. Add the beef, marjoram, oregano, smoked paprika and stir. Pour in the wine and cook for 8 minutes, stirring occasionally. Season with salt and pepper, remove the pan from the heat and cool.

★ Roll out the pastry as thinly as possible on a lightly floured surface, and cut rounds of pastry with the cookie cutter. Gather the leftover pastry and repeat until all the pastry is used up. Put a teaspoon of the filling in the middle of each round. Fold over and seal the edges with a fork. Place them on the prepared baking sheet and brush with the beaten egg.

★ Bake in the oven for 15 minutes until golden brown. Sprinkle with sea salt and serve with the Texan Hot Sauce.

MAPLE-CURED BACON & TOMATO SANDWICH

THERE'S NO TURNING BACK ONCE YOU'VE TRIED HOMEMADE MAPLE-CURED BACON, ALTHOUGH YOU WILL NEED TO PREPARE IT A WEEK IN ADVANCE. WHEN IT'S READY, JUST TRY TO STOP YOURSELF FRYING UP THE WHOLE LOT AND WORKING YOUR WAY THROUGH IT WITH STICKY FINGERS AND GUILTY PLEASURE.

for the maple-cured bacon

140 g/1 cup sea salt

400 g/2 cups brown sugar (preferably dark brown sugar)

320 g/1 cup pure maple syrup

2.25–4.5 kg/5–10 lbs. pork belly, washed and patted dry, with the skin left on

for the sandwich

8 slices sourdough bread

2 tablespoons mayonnaise

4 eggs (optional)

8 tomato slices

4 slices Cheddar cheese (optional)

maple-cured bacon (see above), 2 slices per sandwich

a handful of rocket/arugula

sea salt and freshly ground black pepper

serves 4

★ Curing bacon at home takes a while, but it's really worth it. In a medium bowl, combine the salt, sugar and maple syrup. Rub the mixture over the pork belly on both sides. Put the pork in a large resealable plastic bag with a zip and seal tightly. Refrigerate and leave to cure for 7 days, turning once a day.

★ After 7 days, the bacon will be cured. Cut off a small piece and fry it to test the saltiness of the bacon. If the bacon doesn't taste too salty after being cooked, you are ready to proceed. If the bacon tastes too salty, soak the remaining pork belly in cold water for 1 hour.

★ Once the bacon is ready to cook, carefully slice it into strips of the desired thickness. Fry it for 3–4 minutes per side, until it reaches the crispiness that you like. Fry the eggs, if using.

★ Assemble the sandwiches with slices of sourdough bread, mayonnaise, eggs (if using), tomatoes, Cheddar cheese (if using), rocket/arugula, salt and pepper.

STEAK SANDWICH
with sautéed onions & blue cheese

2 x 350-g/12-oz. sirloin/New York strip steaks, cut 2.5-cm/1-inch thick

olive oil, for frying

4 onions, sliced into rings

½ teaspoon fresh thyme leaves

2 garlic cloves, crushed

1–2 loaves rustic French bread

4 tablespoons Dijonnaise, made by mixing mayonnaise and a little Dijon mustard

30 g/1 cup rocket/arugula

115–225 g/4–8 oz. blue cheese, crumbled

sea salt and freshly ground black pepper

makes 4

A GOOD STEAK SANDWICH ISN'T ALWAYS THE EASIEST TO COME BY. IT'S HARD TO FIND THE RIGHT COMBINATION OF PERFECTLY SPICED STEAK, TOPPED WITH A BOUNTY OF TRIMMINGS THAT ADD THE RIGHT AMOUNT OF FLAVOUR AND TEXTURE WHEN PLACED ON A CRISPY LOAF OF BREAD. THIS SANDWICH, WITH RARE STEAK, SAUTÉED ONIONS, DIJONNAISE, ROCKET/ARUGULA AND BLUE CHEESE ON RUSTIC FRENCH BREAD, IS THE ANSWER!

★ Season the steaks with salt and pepper on both sides. Heat 2–4 tablespoons of olive oil in a medium frying pan/skillet over a high heat until it's very hot, almost smoking. Sear the steaks for 1½ minutes per side and then reduce the heat to low and cook the steaks for about 3–4 minutes, turning once. Remove the steaks from the pan and place on a plate. Cover tightly with foil and allow to sit in the refrigerator for 10 minutes. Remove and slice the steak into strips.

★ Using the same frying pan/skillet, heat 3 tablespoons more olive oil over a medium heat. Add the onion slices and thyme and sauté for 10 minutes, stirring occasionally, until the onion is caramelized. Add the garlic for the last 1–2 minutes.

★ Cut the French bread lengthways and into large sandwich rolls. Spread 1 tablespoon Dijonnaise on the bottom half of each roll. Place a layer of the steak strips on top of the mayonnaise, sprinkle with salt and pepper and top with the caramelized onion rings. Place the rocket/arugula on top of the onion rings and sprinkle a handful of blue cheese on top. Cover with the top half of the rolls and serve.

for the corn & pepper salsa

2 large corn cobs

3 tablespoons vegetable oil

4 spring onions/scallions, sliced

freshly squeezed juice of 1 lime

6 Pepperdew peppers, diced

2 tablespoons finely chopped coriander/cilantro

a dash of chilli/chile sauce

sea salt and freshly ground black pepper

for the sliders

1 tablespoon canned black beans

1 spring onion/scallion, sliced

1 garlic clove, finely chopped

2 teaspoons tomato purée/paste

a pinch of cayenne pepper

1 tablespoon freshly chopped coriander/cilantro

200 g/7 oz. lean minced/ground beef

40 g/3 tablespoons long-grain rice, cooked and cooled

1 tablespoon olive or vegetable oil

a pinch of sea salt and freshly ground black pepper

to serve

4 mini poppyseed rolls

mayonnaise

makes 4 sliders

BEEF & BLACK BEAN SLIDERS
with corn & pepper salsa

CAPTURE THE TASTE OF SOUTH AMERICA WHEREVER YOU ARE WITH THESE SPICY PINT-SIZE BEEF SLIDERS. SERVED WITH HOT CORN AND PEPPER SALSA, THESE ARE GUARANTEED TO CREATE A FIESTA OF FLAVOURS FOR YOUR TASTEBUDS.

★ To make the salsa, cut down the sides of the corn cobs with a sharp knife to remove the kernels. Heat 2 teaspoons of the oil in a frying pan/skillet set over medium heat. Add the corn and cook for 2–3 minutes until it begins to brown. Add the spring onions/scallions and cook for 1 minute. Transfer to a bowl and leave to cool.

★ Add the lime juice, peppers, coriander/cilantro and the remaining oil, and mix well. Add a dash of chilli/chile sauce and season with salt and pepper.

★ To make the sliders, blitz the black beans, spring onion/scallion, garlic, tomato purée/paste, cayenne pepper and coriander/cilantro in a food processor. Pour the mixture into a mixing bowl, add the beef and work together with your hands until evenly mixed. Add the cooled rice, season with salt and pepper and mix again.

★ Divide the beef mixture into quarters and shape into four slider patties. Press each silder down to make them nice and flat.

★ Heat the oil in a frying pan/skillet and fry the sliders over a medium–high heat for 4 minutes on each side until cooked through.

★ Slice the mini poppyseed rolls in half and spread the bottom half of each with mayonnaise. Put a cooked slider on top of each and add a large spoonful of Corn & Pepper Salsa. Finish the sliders with the lids of the rolls.

INDIAN-STYLE LAMB SLIDERS with minted yogurt & mango chutney

CURE THAT CURRY CRAVING WITH THESE DELICIOUSLY SPICED INDIAN-STYLE SLIDERS WHICH PACK A PUNCH. SERVED ON MINI NAAN BREADS, THEY ARE IDEAL AS AN INTERESTING BAR SNACK. THE MINTED YOGURT AND MANGO CHUTNEY OFFSET THE SPICE PERFECTLY.

for the sliders

200 g/7 oz. lean minced/ground lamb

1 tablespoon garam masala

a pinch of ground turmeric

3 tablespoons fresh breadcrumbs

1 tablespoon beaten egg

a pinch of freshly chopped coriander/cilantro

a pinch of sea salt and freshly ground black pepper

to serve

4 mini naan breads

plain yogurt mixed with freshly chopped mint leaves

mango chutney

cocktail sticks/toothpicks (optional)

makes 4 sliders

★ Put the lamb in a bowl with the garam masala, turmeric, breadcrumbs, egg, coriander/cilantro and salt and pepper. Divide the mixture into quarters and shape into four slider patties. Press each slider down to make them nice and flat.

★ Heat the oil in a frying pan/skillet and fry the sliders over medium–high heat for 4 minutes on each side until cooked through.

★ Splash a little water on each of the mini naan breads and toast under the grill/broiler or in a toaster to warm. Put a generous spoonful of minted yogurt over the top of each mini naan. Top with a cooked slider and finish with a spoonful of mango chutney. Put a cocktail stick/toothpick through the middle of each, if needed, and serve.

for the pickle relish

225 g/1 cup Sweet & Sour Cherry Pickles (see page 21), chopped

1 small white onion, chopped

3 garlic cloves, crushed

1 teaspoon sugar

¼ teaspoon sea salt

for the sliders

450–680 g/1–1½ lbs. extra lean minced/ground beef

2 spring onions/scallions, diced

1 teaspoon sea salt

1 teaspoon freshly ground black pepper

½ tablespoon olive oil

1 egg

for the secret sauce

115 g/½ cup mayonnaise

2 tablespoons creamy French dressing

3 tablespoons Pickle Relish (see above)

½ small white onion, finely diced

1 teaspoon vinegar

1 teaspoon granulated sugar

a pinch of sea salt

to serve

8–12 slices American or Cheddar cheese

8–12 slider buns

iceberg lettuce, cut into strips

gherkins, sliced

makes 8–12

SLIDERS with secret sauce

POPULARIZED IN NEW YORK IN THE 1990S, THESE TASTY MINI-BURGERS ARE THE QUINTESSENTIAL AMERICAN SNACK AND WILL NEVER FAIL TO BRING A SMILE TO YOUR FACE! NOT AS FILLING AS REGULAR-SIZE BURGERS BUT JUST RIGHT FOR A QUICK FIX.

★ Make the Pickle Relish in advance, by mixing all the ingredients in a bowl and storing in a jar or Tupperware container to marinade for at least 24 hours.

★ In a medium mixing bowl, combine the minced/ground beef, diced spring onions/scallions, salt, pepper, olive oil and egg. Mix well with your hands and then press the meat mixture into patties. You can use a cookie cutter to get even and equal-sized sliders. This recipe makes 8–12 sliders depending on the size you prefer.

★ In a small mixing bowl, combine the secret sauce ingredients and season to taste.

★ Cook the sliders on a grill/broiler or pan-fry them to your liking. Place a slice of cheese on top of the hot slider to let it melt a little. Meanwhile, cut the slider buns in half and spread the secret sauce on the bottom half. Chop the iceberg lettuce into strips and place a few on top of the sauce. Put the slider and cheese on top, followed by more secret sauce and a couple of sliced gherkins. Add the top half of the bun.

★ Serve the sliders warm with sliced gherkins on the side.

12–16 preserved vine leaves (see right), plus a few extra to line the pot

1–2 tablespoons olive oil

1 onion, finely chopped

2 garlic cloves, finely chopped

1 tablespoon pine nuts

1 tablespoon tiny currants, soaked in boiling water for 10 minutes and drained

1 teaspoon ground allspice

1 teaspoon ground cinnamon

150 g/¾ cup short-grain or risotto rice, well rinsed and drained

sea salt and freshly ground black pepper

a small bunch of fresh flat-leaf parsley, finely chopped

a small bunch of fresh dill, finely chopped

a small bunch of fresh mint, finely chopped

for the cooking liquid

100 ml/⅔ cup olive oil

freshly squeezed juice of 1 lemon

1 teaspoon caster/granulated sugar

serves 4

VINE LEAVES STUFFED WITH AROMATIC RICE

THIS POPULAR MEZZE DISH IS TRADITIONALLY SERVED AT ROOM TEMPERATURE WITH HOT MELTED BUTTER. PRESERVED VINE LEAVES CAN BE PURCHASED FROM SPECIALITY STORES AND ONLINE.

★ To prepare the preserved vine leaves, put them in a deep bowl and pour over boiling water. Leave them to soak for 15–20 minutes, using a fork to gently separate the leaves. Drain and put them back in the bowl with cold water. Soak for 3 minutes to get rid of any residue, then drain thoroughly. Stack on a plate, cover with a clean, damp tea/dish towel to keep them moist, and put aside.

★ Heat the oil in a heavy-based pan and stir in the onion and garlic, until they begin to colour. Stir in the pine nuts for 1–2 minutes, until they turn golden. Add the currants and when they plump up, stir in the spices. Toss in the rice, making sure it is coated in the spices, and pour in enough water to just cover the rice. Season with salt and pepper and bring the water to a boil. Reduce the heat and cook for about 10 minutes until all the water has been absorbed and the rice is still firm. Toss in the fresh herbs and leave the rice to cool.

★ Place a vine leaf on a plate or board and put a heaped teaspoon of rice at the bottom of the leaf, where the stem would have been. Fold the stem edge over the filling, then fold both of the side edges in towards the middle of the leaf, so that the filling is sealed in. Now roll the leaf up like a small fat cigar. Place the stuffed vine leaf in the palm of your hand and squeeze it lightly to fix the shape. Put aside and repeat with the remaining leaves.

★ In a bowl, mix together the cooking liquid ingredients with 7 tablespoons of water. Line the bottom of a shallow pan with the extra vine leaves, then place the stuffed vine leaves on top, tightly packed side by side. Pour the olive oil mixture over the stuffed vine leaves and place a plate on top of them to prevent them from unravelling during cooking. Cover the pan and simmer gently for 1 hour, topping up the cooking liquid if necessary. Leave the stuffed vine leaves to cool, then lift them out, arrange on a baking sheet and serve.

2 carrots, peeled, halved and cut into long slices

2 courgettes/zucchini, halved and cut into long strips

6–8 cauliflower florets

3–4 spring onions/scallions, trimmed and halved

sunflower oil, for deep frying

for the batter

1 teaspoon dried yeast granules

1 scant teaspoon caster/granulated sugar

3 tablespoons warm water

175 g/1¼ cups plus 1 tablespoon chickpea/gram flour

1 tablespoon ground turmeric

sea salt

2 tablespoons thick, creamy yogurt

200 ml/¾ cup plus 1 tablespoon water

for the garlic yogurt dip

6 heaped tablespoons thick, creamy yogurt

2 garlic cloves, crushed

sea salt and freshly ground black pepper

1–2 tablespoons tomato ketchup

serves 4–6

CRISPY VEGETABLES FRIED IN TURMERIC BATTER

with garlic yogurt dip

A DEEP-FRIED SNACK WITH A MIDDLE EASTERN TWIST, THESE CRISPY VEGETABLES ARE A DELICIOUSLY MOREISH TREAT. YOU CAN USE ANY VEGETABLES OF YOUR CHOICE, INCLUDING THIN SLICES OF PUMPKIN, BUTTERNUT SQUASH, BROCCOLI, (BELL) PEPPERS, AND WHOLE CHILLIES/CHILES. SIMPLY ADJUST THE QUANTITIES ACCORDINGLY. A POPULAR ACCOMPANIMENT FOR DEEP-FRIED VEGETABLES, FALAFEL AND MEZZE FARE IN GENERAL IS A GARLIC-FLAVOURED YOGURT COMBINED WITH A LITTLE TOMATO KETCHUP, WHICH IS INCLUDED HERE.

★ First, prepare the batter. In a small bowl, combine the yeast and sugar with the 3 tablespoons warm water and leave it to froth. Sift the flour and turmeric with a pinch of salt into a bowl, make a well in the middle and tip in the creamed yeast with the yogurt and the 200 ml/¾ cup plus 1 tablespoon warm water. Using a balloon whisk, combine the mixture to form a smooth batter, and leave it to stand for 30 minutes.

★ Meanwhile, prepare the dip. In a small bowl, beat together the yogurt and garlic and season with salt and pepper. Beat in the ketchup.

★ Heat enough sunflower oil for deep frying in a heavy-based frying pan/skillet or wok to 180°C (350°F). Alternatively, use an electric deep fryer. Dip the sliced vegetables and florets into the batter, one at a time, and slip them into the hot oil. Fry them in batches until crisp and golden brown – some will take longer than others – and drain them on paper towels.

★ Tip the crispy fried vegetables onto a serving dish and enjoy dipping them into the creamy ketchup dip!

SHRIMP BAKED WITH TOMATOES & CHEESE

THIS IS A POPULAR MEZZE DISH AROUND THE AEGEAN AND THE EASTERN MEDITERRANEAN.

2–3 tablespoons olive oil

1 onion, cut in half lengthways and finely sliced

1 green (bell) pepper, deseeded and finely sliced

2–3 garlic cloves, finely chopped

1 fresh red chilli/chile, deseeded and finely chopped

1–2 teaspoons coriander seeds

1–2 teaspoons caster/granulated sugar

2 x 400-g/14-oz. cans chopped tomatoes, drained

2 teaspoons white wine vinegar

a small bunch of fresh flat-leaf parsley, chopped

sea salt and freshly ground black pepper

500 g/1 lb. 2 oz. fresh, shelled prawns/shrimp, thoroughly cleaned and drained

120 g/1½ cups grated/shredded firm, tangy cheese, such as Parmesan, Pecorino or mature/sharp Cheddar

serves 4

★ Preheat the oven to 180°C (350°F) Gas 4.

★ Heat the oil in a heavy-based pan. Stir in the onion, (bell) pepper, garlic, chilli/chile and coriander seeds for 2–3 minutes. Add the sugar with the tomatoes and the vinegar, reduce the heat and cook gently for 15–20 minutes, until the mixture resembles a thick sauce.

★ Stir in the parsley and season well with salt and pepper. Toss the prawns/shrimp in the tomato sauce to coat them, then spoon the mixture into individual pots or into an ovenproof dish. Sprinkle the cheese over each one and put them in the preheated oven for 15 minutes, until lightly browned on top.

DEEP-FRIED WHITEBAIT
with lemon

IN THE COASTAL REGIONS OF GREECE, TURKEY AND EASTERN MEDITERRANEAN COUNTRIES, THESE TINY DEEP-FRIED FISH ARE A GREAT FAVOURITE. EATEN WHOLE WITH A SQUEEZE OF LEMON, THEY ARE TRULY DELICIOUS.

500 g/1 lb. 2 oz. fresh whitebait

sunflower oil, for frying

4 tablespoons plain/all-purpose flour

1 scant teaspoon smoked paprika

sea salt, plus extra to serve

a bunch of fresh flat-leaf parsley, finely chopped

1–2 lemons, cut into wedges, to serve

serves 4

★ Wash and drain the fish well – if they are fresh and tiny there should be no need for any other preparation. However, if you have substituted them with a slightly larger fish, you will need to scale and gut them.

★ Heat enough sunflower oil for deep frying in a heavy-based pan. Alternatively, use an electric deep fryer. Combine the flour, smoked paprika and salt and toss the whitebait in the mixture, coating them in the flour, but shake off any excess. Fry the fish in batches for 2–3 minutes, until crispy and golden. Drain on paper towels.

★ Transfer the whitebait to a serving dish or plate, sprinkle with extra salt and gently toss in the parsley. Serve with lemon wedges.

LITTLE SPINACH & FETA PASTRIES
with pine nuts

THE VARIETY OF SAVOURY AND SWEET PASTRIES IN THE MIDDLE EAST IS ENDLESS, PARTICULARLY IN THE EASTERN MEDITERRANEAN REGION AND MOROCCO. THE SAVOURY ONES ARE GENERALLY PREPARED WITH PUFF AND FLAKY PASTRY DOUGHS, SUCH AS IN THIS DELICIOUS SPINACH AND CHEESE SNACK, WHICH IS PERFECT FOR ANY TIME OF DAY OR NIGHT.

500 g/1 lb. 2 oz. fresh spinach leaves, trimmed, washed and drained

2 tablespoons olive oil

1 tablespoon butter

2 onions, chopped

3 generous tablespoons pine nuts

freshly squeezed juice of 1 lemon

1 teaspoon ground allspice

150 g/5 oz. feta, crumbled

a small bunch of fresh dill, finely chopped

sea salt and freshly ground black pepper

plain/all-purpose flour, for dusting

450 g/16 oz. ready-prepared puff pastry, thawed if frozen

extra olive oil, for brushing

10-cm/4-inch round pastry cutter
2 baking sheets lined with foil

serves 6

★ Preheat the oven to 180°C (350°F) Gas 4.

★ Steam the spinach until it has softened, then drain and refresh under cold running water before squeezing out the excess liquid with your hands. Put the spinach on a wooden board and chop it coarsely.

★ Heat the oil and butter in a heavy-based frying pan/skillet and stir in the onion to soften. Add 2 tablespoons of the pine nuts and cook for 2–3 minutes until both the onions and pine nuts begin to turn golden. Stir in the spinach with the lemon juice and allspice and lightly fold in the crumbled feta and dill. Season the mixture and leave to cool.

★ On a lightly floured work surface roll the pastry into a thin sheet. Using a pastry cutter or the rim of a cup, cut out as many 10-cm/4-inch rounds as you can and pile them up, lightly dusting them with flour. Take each round and spoon a little of the spinach mixture in the middle. Pull up the sides to make a pyramid by pinching the edges with your fingertips. It does not matter if one of the sides opens during cooking to reveal the filling; that is part of their appeal.

★ Place the pastries on the prepared baking sheets. Brush the tops with a little oil and bake them in the preheated oven for about 30 minutes, until golden brown.

★ Roughly 5 minutes before taking the pastries out of the oven, spread the remaining tablespoon of pine nuts onto a small piece of aluminium foil and toast them in the oven until they turn golden brown. Once you have placed the little pastries on a plate, sprinkle the toasted pine nuts over them and serve while they are still hot.

DEEP-FRIED MUSSELS IN BEER BATTER with garlicky walnut sauce

100 g/¾ cup plain/all-purpose flour

1 teaspoon sea salt

½ teaspoon bicarbonate of soda/baking soda

2 egg yolks

150 ml/⅔ cup light beer

20 fresh, shelled mussels, thoroughly cleaned

sunflower oil, for deep frying

for the garlicky walnut sauce

100 g/¾ cup walnuts

2 small slices day-old white bread, with crusts removed, soaked in a little water and squeezed dry

2 garlic cloves, crushed

3 tablespoons olive oil

freshly squeezed juice of 1 lemon

1 teaspoon runny honey

a dash of white wine vinegar

sea salt and freshly ground black pepper

wooden skewers

serves 4

GREAT STREET FOOD IN THE PORTS OF ISTANBUL, IZMIR AND BEIRUT, AND CLASSIC MEZZE IN COASTAL MEDITERRANEAN REGIONS, FRESHLY PICKED MUSSELS ARE SHELLED, DIPPED IN BATTER AND FRIED IN A HUGE, CURVED PAN, SIMILAR TO A LARGE WOK. THE GOLDEN, CRISPY-COATED, JUICY MUSSELS ARE OFTEN PUSHED ONTO STICKS AND SERVED WITH A GARLICKY BREAD, OR NUT, SAUCE – YOU CAN USE PISTACHIOS, ALMONDS OR PINE NUTS. THE SAME IDEA CAN BE APPLIED TO FRESH, SHELLED PRAWNS/SHRIMP OR STRIPS OF SQUID.

★ To make the batter, sift the flour, salt and bicarbonate of soda/baking soda into a bowl. Make a well in the middle and drop in the egg yolks. Gradually pour in the beer, using a wooden spoon to draw in the flour from the sides. Beat well until thick and smooth. Put aside for 30 minutes.

★ Meanwhile, make the sauce. Using a pestle and mortar, pound the walnuts to a paste, or whizz them in an electric blender. Add the bread and garlic and pound to a paste. Drizzle in the olive oil, stirring all the time, and beat in the lemon juice and honey. Add the dash of vinegar and season well with salt and pepper (the sauce should be creamy, so add more olive oil or a little water if it is too thick). Spoon the sauce into a serving bowl.

★ Heat enough oil for deep frying in a heavy-based pan or wok. Alternatively use an electric deep fryer. Using your fingers, dip each mussel into the batter and drop them into the oil. Fry them in batches until golden brown and drain on paper towels.

★ Thread the mussels onto small wooden skewers and serve immediately with the sauce for dipping.

500 ml/2¼ cups dried chickpeas

1 onion, quartered

2 teaspoons sea salt

a pinch of freshly ground black pepper

2–3 garlic cloves

2–3 slices stale bread

3 tablespoons fresh flat-leaf parsley, finely chopped

⅓ red (bell) pepper

2 teaspoons ground cumin

2 teaspoons ground coriander

1 teaspoon chilli/hot red pepper flakes

2 tablespoons plain/all-purpose flour

2 teaspoons baking powder

1 litre/quart vegetable oil, for deep frying

for the taratoor sauce

175 ml/¾ cup tahini

freshly squeezed juice of 2 lemons

1 garlic clove, crushed

1 teaspoon sea salt

a handful of fresh flat-leaf parsley, finely chopped, plus extra to serve

to serve

8 pitta breads, toasted

a few cos/romaine lettuce leaves

2 tomatoes, sliced

fresh mint leaves

4 pickled gherkins

an electric deep fryer (optional)

serves 4

FALAFEL

TO MOST PEOPLE, FALAFEL ARE THE SORT OF TREAT THAT CAN BE ENJOYED WITHOUT REMORSE OR SHAME. THEY ARE THE PERFECT COMBINATION OF GOOD AND BAD. THE GOOD SIDE IS THAT THEY'RE MADE WITH CHICKPEAS, SO ARE LOW IN FAT AS WELL AS FILLING AND DELICIOUS. THE BAD SIDE IS THAT THEY'RE FRIED – BUT THIS ISN'T EXACTLY A HEALTHY FOOD COOKBOOK, SO ENJOY!

★ Soak the dried chickpeas in a large bowl of cold water for at least 12 hours.

★ Drain the chickpeas and add to a food processor, along with the onion, salt, black pepper, garlic, bread, parsley, red (bell) pepper and spices. Blend until it reaches a granular consistency. Add the flour, baking powder and 175 ml/¾ cup water and mix well.

★ Moisten your hands and form small balls of the chickpea mixture and flatten them slightly.

★ Heat the vegetable oil in a deep fryer or a large frying pan/skillet to 190°C (375°F) or until the oil is bubbling steadily. Fry the chickpea balls until golden brown. Remove the falafel and drain carefully using paper towels.

★ For the taratoor sauce, in a deep bowl, beat the tahini with the lemon juice and crushed garlic until it becomes quite creamy. Add 175ml/¾ cup water little by little, and continue to beat well. Add the salt and parsley and stir. Taste and if the sauce isn't tangy enough, add a little more lemon juice. Refrigerate until ready to use.

★ To serve, stuff a couple of lettuce leaves into each pitta bread and add 2–3 falafel. Add the tomato slices, parsley and mint. Drizzle on the sauce and serve with pickled gherkins.

BAKED DATES STUFFED WITH HARISSA COUSCOUS

110 g/⅔ cup dried couscous

½ teaspoon sea salt

150 ml/½ cup plus 2 tablespoons warm water

2 tablespoons olive oil

1 teaspoon harissa paste

1 teaspoon runny honey

4–6 ready-to-eat dried apricots, finely chopped

a small bunch of fresh coriander/cilantro, finely chopped

12 large, ready-to-eat Medjool dates

freshly squeezed juice of 1 lemon or 1 small orange

2 tablespoons butter

2 tablespoons whole blanched almonds

serves 4–6

DATES CAN BE ENJOYED IN BOTH THEIR FRESH AND DRIED FORMS, POUNDED TO A PASTE AND SIMMERED INTO SYRUP. IT'S NO WONDER THAT THEY HAVE FOUND THEIR WAY INTO MANY SWEET AND SAVOURY RECIPES LIKE THIS MEZZE DISH, WHICH IS DISTINCTLY MOROCCAN IN CHARACTER.

★ Preheat the oven to 180°C (350°F) Gas 4.

★ Tip the couscous into a bowl. Stir the salt into the water and pour it over the couscous. Stir to make sure the water is absorbed evenly, then cover the bowl with a dampened tea/dish towel and leave the couscous to swell for about 10 minutes.

★ Rake the couscous with a fork to separate the grains and rub a tablespoon of the oil into them, aerating them with your fingertips. Rub in the harissa and honey and toss in the chopped apricots and the coriander/cilantro.

★ Using a small sharp knife, slit the dates down one side to extract the stone and fill the cavity with the couscous, stuffing it in gently. Place the dates side by side in a baking dish and drizzle the remaining tablespoon of olive oil over them combined with the lemon or orange juice. Cover the dish with foil and put them in the preheated oven for 25 minutes to heat through.

★ Meanwhile, melt the butter in a small saucepan and stir in the almonds, until they are golden brown. Lift the almonds out of the butter and separate into halves.

★ Arrange the stuffed dates on a serving dish and garnish each one with a halved, buttered almond. Drizzle a little of the almond butter over the top and serve while still warm.

250 g/3 cups grated courgette/zucchini

4 spring onions/scallions, finely sliced

grated zest and freshly squeezed juice of 1 lemon

1 teaspoon vegetable oil, plus extra for deep-frying

3 tablespoons chickpea/gram flour

1 teaspoon baking powder

sea salt

for the minted yogurt dip

½ cucumber, deseeded and grated

200 g/1 cup thick plain yogurt

½ garlic clove, crushed

a handful of fresh mint, chopped

a squeeze of fresh lemon juice

½ teaspoon caster/granulated sugar

sea salt and freshly ground black pepper

an electric deep fryer

serves 4

COURGETTE/ZUCCHINI FRITTERS with minted yogurt dip

THESE FRITTERS ARE PERFECT FOR ENJOYING WITH DRINKS. THEY TASTE GREAT WITH COURGETTES/ZUCCHINI BUT YOU CAN USE CARROTS, BEET(ROOT) OR ONIONS, IF PREFERRED. AND YOU CAN ADD FETA, HERBS, SPICES AND CHILLI/CHILE FOR EXTRA FLAVOUR – JUST EXPERIMENT WITH WHATEVER YOU FIND AT HOME.

★ To make the Minted Yogurt Dip, put the grated cucumber in a strainer set over a bowl and leave for 10 minutes to drain any excess liquid. Alternatively you can squeeze out any liquid in a clean tea/dish towel. Put the drained grated cucumber in a bowl with the yogurt. Add and stir in the crushed garlic and the chopped mint. Add a squeeze of lemon juice, sugar and season well with salt and pepper. Taste and adjust the seasoning with more lemon juice, sugar or salt if necessary.

★ To make the fritters, sprinkle the courgette/zucchini with salt and put it in a strainer set over a bowl for 10 minutes to draw out any moisture. Alternatively you can squeeze out any liquid in a clean tea/dish towel.

★ Put the drained grated courgette/zucchini in a bowl, add the spring onions/scallions, lemon zest and juice and teaspoon of vegetable oil, and stir until thoroughly mixed. Combine the flour and baking powder, sprinkle them over the vegetables, then stir until well combined.

★ These fritters are best made in a deep fryer, set to 180°C (350°F). If you don't have a deep fryer, put about 2 cm/¾ inch of oil in the bottom of a wok. Heat the oil until hot but not smoking. Drop teaspoons of mixture into the oil and cook for about 2 minutes until crisp and golden.

★ Remove the fritters with a slotted spoon and drain on paper towels. Sprinkle them with sea salt while they are still hot. The fritters are best served immediately but will keep for a short time in a warm oven.

LAMB KOFTES with tahini yogurt dip

1 kg/3 lbs. minced/ground lamb

1½ teaspoons ground cumin

1½ teaspoons sweet paprika

1 teaspoon ground allspice

1 teaspoon chilli/chili powder

150 g/1 cup (about 1 medium) finely diced red onion

25 g/½ cup fresh flat-leaf parsley, finely chopped

40 g/¾ cup fresh coriander/cilantro, finely chopped, plus extra to serve

freshly squeezed juice and grated zest of 1 lemon, plus wedges to serve

3 large eggs

1 teaspoon sea salt

60 ml/¼ cup sunflower oil, for frying

for the tahini yogurt dip

250 ml/1 cup Greek yogurt

25 ml/2 tablespoons tahini paste

2 tablespoons freshly squeezed lemon juice

10 g/¼ cup fresh mint, finely chopped

¼ cucumber, grated

1 garlic clove, crushed

½ teaspoon sea salt, or to taste

to serve

fresh coriander/cilantro, roughly chopped

lemon wedges

30 x 15-cm/6-inch wooden skewers, soaked in water for at least 30 minutes

makes 30 skewers

THESE SPICED LAMB SKEWERS ARE A PARTICULARLY TEMPTING (YET CLASSY) LATE-NIGHT OFFERING. KEEP THEM NICE AND JUICY BY NOT OVERCOOKING THE LAMB. IT IS REALLY WORTH WHIPPING UP THE SMOOTH TAHINI YOGURT DIP TO ACCOMPANY THEM.

★ To make the koftes, put all of the ingredients except the oil in a large mixing bowl and mix everything together using your hands.

★ Shape the kofte mixture around each of the soaked skewers (about 45–50 g/1½–2 oz. per skewer) in a sausage shape and press the mixture firmly together. Transfer to a baking sheet, cover with clingfilm/plastic wrap and set in the fridge for at least 2 hours, or preferably overnight, to firm up.

★ Preheat the oven to 180°C (350°F) Gas 4.

★ Heat the sunflower oil in a large frying pan/skillet set over a medium–high heat. Add the koftes in batches and cook for about 4 minutes, turning them until golden brown all over. Transfer to a clean baking sheet, while you cook the remaining koftes in the same way, adding more oil to the pan each time if necessary.

★ When all the koftes have been fried, place them in the preheated oven for 5 minutes to cook through.

★ To make the Tahini Yogurt Dip, mix all the ingredients together and season with salt to taste.

★ Serve the koftes on a platter scattered with chopped coriander/cilantro, with lemon wedges and the Tahini Yogurt Dip on the side.

PERSIAN SAUSAGE ROLLS

375 g/13 oz. ready-rolled puff pastry

1 egg, beaten

for the sausage mix

1 tablespoon olive oil

½ red onion, finely chopped

400 g/14 oz. sausage meat

45 g/1½ oz. chopped pistachios

25 g/1 oz. barberries

½ teaspoon sumac

½ teaspoon freshly ground black pepper

½ teaspoon ground cinnamon

½ teaspoon ground cumin

a baking sheet, lined with baking parchment

makes 20–25

★ First make the sausage mix. Heat the oil in a frying pan/skillet. Add the onion and sauté until caramelized. Cool and mix well with all of the other ingredients.

★ Lay the pastry sheet on a lightly floured surface and give it a little roll, if necessary, to make it 3-mm/⅛-inch thick. Cut it crossways into 3 strips.

★ Divide the sausage meat into 3 parts and press a line of sausage meat down the middle of each strip of pastry, leaving 2.5 cm/1 inch free at each end.

★ Brush the length of the pastry with a little beaten egg on one side and roll the other side over the sausage to secure it in place. Pinch the ends of each roll together.

★ Transfer the rolls to the prepared baking sheet, brush them with more egg wash and pop them in the freezer for 15 minutes. Meanwhile, preheat the oven to 190°C (375°F) Gas 5.

★ Cut each sausage roll into 8 pieces.

★ If you have leftover egg wash, brush it on, spread the rolls out on the prepared baking sheet and bake for at least 20 minutes, or until golden.

MOROCCAN CHICKEN PUFFS

500 g/1 lb. 2 oz. puff pastry

1 egg, beaten

sesame seeds, for sprinkling

for the chicken mix

2 tablespoons olive oil

1 large onion, finely chopped

3 garlic cloves, crushed

½ teaspoon ground ginger

¼ teaspoon ground cinnamon

a small pinch of saffron

¼ teaspoon ground cumin

1 small preserved lemon, quartered, seeds and pith removed

4 chicken thighs, boned, skinned and very finely diced

¼ teaspoon smoked paprika

freshly ground black pepper

1 tablespoon freshly chopped flat-leaf parsley

1 tablespoon freshly chopped coriander/cilantro

7.5-cm/3-inch cookie cutter

a baking sheet, lined with baking parchment

makes 30–35

★ Preheat the oven to 180°C (350°F) Gas 4.

★ For the chicken mix, heat the oil in a frying pan/skillet and sauté the onion and garlic for 5 minutes. Add the other chicken mix ingredients, except the seasoning and herbs. When the chicken is cooked, cool for a few minutes before seasoning with black pepper and adding the fresh herbs. Leave to cool completely.

★ Roll out the puff pastry until 3-mm/⅛-inch thick and use the cookie cutter to cut it into rounds.

★ Place 1 teaspoonful of the chicken mix in the middle of each disk and then pinch the edges together, like a dumpling. Place the puffs pinch-side down on the prepared baking sheet 2.5 cm/1 inch apart and brush the tops with the beaten egg. Sprinkle with sesame seeds and bake for 15–20 minutes until golden.

EGG ROLLS

THERE IS SOMETHING SO SATISFYING ABOUT AN EGG ROLL. MAYBE IT'S THE CRUNCH; MAYBE IT'S THE TEXTURE; MAYBE IT'S SOMETHING ABOUT HOW PORK AND CABBAGE COME TOGETHER SO WELL WHEN HUGGED BETWEEN EGG ROLL WRAPPERS AND DEEP FRIED. WHATEVER IT IS, THEY'RE ONE OF THE MOST DELICIOUS BAR SNACKS OUT THERE!

3 tablespoons olive oil

1 teaspoon sea salt

1 teaspoon freshly ground black pepper

1 teaspoon ground ginger

1 teaspoon garlic powder

450 g/1 lb. pork shoulder

1 litre/quart peanut oil, for frying

2 tablespoons plain/all-purpose flour

120 g/2 cups cabbage, shredded

1 medium carrot, shredded

8 x 18-cm/7-inch square egg roll wrappers

2 tablespoons sesame seeds (optional)

for the sweet and sour sauce

1 tablespoon soy sauce

3½ tablespoons caster/superfine sugar

3½ tablespoons white vinegar

zest of 1 unwaxed orange

a meat thermometer

makes 8

★ Preheat the oven to 180°C (350°F) Gas 4.

★ Spread the oil, salt, ground black pepper, ginger and garlic powder on the pork shoulder.

★ Set the meat on a rack set into a roasting pan. Roast for 20 minutes, and then reduce the heat to 160°C (325°F) Gas 3. Continue to cook until a meat thermometer inserted into the shoulder reads 85°C (185°F), about 1–2 hours. Remove the pork from the oven and leave to stand until cool enough to handle, about 30 minutes. Shred the pork.

★ Combine the flour with 2 tablespoons water in a bowl until they form a paste. In a separate bowl combine the cabbage, carrots and shredded pork and mix them together.

★ Lay out one egg roll wrapper with a corner pointed towards you. Place about 20 g/¼ cup of the cabbage, carrot and shredded pork mixture onto the wrapper and fold the corner up over the mixture. Fold the left and right corners towards the centre and continue to roll. Brush a bit of the flour paste on the final corner to help seal.

★ In a large frying pan/skillet or deep fryer heat the peanut oil to about 190°C (375°F). Place the egg rolls into the heated oil and fry, turning occasionally, until golden brown. Remove from oil and drain on paper towels or a wire rack. Put on a serving plate and top with sesame seeds, if desired.

★ To make the Sweet and Sour Sauce, mix all the ingredients together in a mixing bowl with 1 tablespoon water. Transfer to a small saucepan and bring to a boil, then remove from the heat. Pour the sauce into a small bowl ready to dip the egg rolls into.

VIETNAMESE SPRING ROLLS

VERY DIFFERENT FROM CHINESE SPRING ROLLS, WHICH ARE DEEP-FRIED, THE VIETNAMESE SERVE SPRING ROLLS ENCASED IN LIGHT, TRANSLUCENT RICE WRAPPERS. THIS MEANS YOU CAN MAKE OUT THE DELICIOUSLY FRESH-TASTING, FRAGRANT CONTENTS INSIDE. THERE ARE MANY DIFFERENT NAMES FOR THE VIETNAMESE SPRING ROLL, INCLUDING SALAD ROLL, SUMMER ROLL AND CRYSTAL ROLL.

55 g/2 oz. rice vermicelli

8 rice wrappers (each one 21.5 cm/8½ inches in diameter)

4–6 shiitake mushrooms, cut into matchsticks

115 g/½ cup medium to firm tofu, sliced into matchstick pieces

30 g/½ cup cabbage, shredded or finely chopped

1½ tablespoons fresh Thai basil, chopped

3 tablespoons fresh mint leaves, chopped

3 tablespoons fresh coriander/cilantro, chopped

2 lettuce leaves of choice, chopped

4 teaspoons fish sauce

2 tablespoons freshly squeezed lime juice

1 garlic clove, crushed

2 tablespoons caster/granulated sugar

½ teaspoon garlic chilli/chile sauce

3 tablespoons hoisin sauce

1 teaspoon peanuts, finely chopped

makes 8

★ Bring a medium saucepan of water to a boil. Boil the rice vermicelli for 3–5 minutes, or until al dente, and drain.

★ Fill a large bowl with hot water. Dip one rice wrapper into the hot water for 1 second to soften. Lay the wrapper flat. In a row across the centre of the wrapper, place 1 tablespoon of shiitake, 1 tablespoon tofu, a handful of cabbage, a little basil, mint, coriander/cilantro and lettuce, leaving about 5 cm/2 inches uncovered on each side. Fold the uncovered sides inward, then tightly roll the wrapper, beginning at the end with the lettuce. Repeat to make another 7 spring rolls.

★ In a small bowl, mix together the fish sauce with 60 ml/¼ cup water, lime juice, garlic, sugar and garlic chilli/chile sauce. In another small bowl, mix together the hoisin sauce and peanuts.

★ Serve the spring rolls at room temperature and dip them into both sauces at will!

SESAME SHRIMP TOASTS

10 slices (slightly stale) white bread, crusts removed

30–40 fresh coriander/cilantro leaves, to garnish

5 tablespoons sesame seeds

400 ml/1¾ cups groundnut/peanut or vegetable oil

plum or sweet chilli/chile sauce, to serve

for the topping

6 spring onions/scallions, roughly chopped

450 g/1 lb. raw prawns/shrimp, peeled and deveined

1 teaspoon freshly chopped coriander/cilantro

1 garlic clove, crushed

1 tablespoon grated fresh ginger

1 egg white

2 teaspoons soy sauce

1 tablespoon cornflour/cornstarch

makes 30

★ For the topping, whizz the spring onions/scallions in a food processor. Add the other ingredients and whizz again.

★ Spread the topping onto each slice of bread. Sprinkle the sesame seeds on a plate and gently press each slice of bread, prawn-/shrimp-side down, into the seeds. Cut each slice into three fingers and press a coriander/cilantro leaf into one end.

★ Heat the oil in frying pan/skillet. Cook the toast topping-side down for a couple of minutes. Flip over and cook for 40 seconds more, until crisp. Drain on paper towels. Serve with plum or sweet chilli/chile sauce.

YELLOW BEAN SHRIMP

2 tablespoons vegetable oil

3 garlic cloves, finely chopped

1 fresh red chilli/chile, deseeded and finely chopped

2.5-cm/1-inch piece of fresh ginger, grated

20 raw king prawns/jumbo shrimp, peeled and deveined, with tails left on

3 tablespoons yellow bean sauce

1 tablespoon Shaoxing rice wine or dry sherry

1 tablespoon caster/granulated sugar

1 fresh red chilli/chile, sliced, to garnish

makes 20

★ Heat the oil in a wok or large frying pan/skillet over a high heat. Add the garlic, chilli/chile and ginger. After 10 seconds, add the prawns/shrimp and toss to combine. Add the yellow bean sauce, wine or sherry, 1 tablespoon water and the sugar.

★ After 4 minutes, check a prawn/shrimp to see if it is cooked. Scatter with sliced fresh chilli/chile and serve.

DEVILLED EGGS WITH SHRIMP

12 hard-boiled/hard-cooked eggs, peeled

4 tablespoons mayonnaise

1–2 tablespoons chilli/chile shrimp paste

sea salt and ground white pepper

2 spring onions/scallions

1 teaspoon black sesame seeds, to serve

piping/pastry bag with star-shaped nozzle/tip (optional)

makes 24

★ Halve the eggs lengthways and remove the yolks. Put the yolks into a bowl and break them up with a fork.

★ Mix in the mayonnaise and chilli/chile shrimp paste to taste. Season with salt and white pepper. When smooth, either spoon back into the eggs or pipe with a star-shaped nozzle/tip, if you have one.

★ Sprinkle over the sliced spring onions/scallions and black sesame seeds and serve.

THAI-STYLE MINI FISH CAKES

with cucumber & peanut dipping sauce

THESE SPICY LITTLE FISH CAKES CAN BE PREPARED AND COOKED IN ADVANCE, THEN REHEATED COVERED WITH FOIL UNTIL PIPING HOT IN AN OVEN ON A MEDIUM HEAT. THEY ARE GREAT SERVED ALONGSIDE THE VIETNAMESE SPRING ROLLS (SEE PAGE 96). SQUEEZE A LITTLE LIME OVER BEFORE SERVING WITH THE SPICY, NUTTY DIPPING SAUCE.

125 g/4 oz. skinless, boneless cod or other white fish

150 g/5 oz. raw prawns/shrimp, peeled and deveined

100 g/1 cup grated fresh coconut

1 fresh red chilli/chile

4 spring onions/scallions, sliced

1 tablespoon freshly chopped coriander/cilantro

1 tablespoon Thai red curry paste

a pinch of sea salt

2–3 tablespoons sunflower oil, for frying

lime wedges, to serve

for the cucumber & peanut dipping sauce

125 ml/½ cup rice wine vinegar

100 g/½ cup caster/granulated sugar

1 fresh red chilli/chile, finely chopped

1 carrot

3-cm/1-inch piece of cucumber

1 tablespoon roasted peanuts

serves 2–4

★ Prepare the dipping sauce first. Pour the vinegar into a small saucepan, add the sugar and bring slowly to a boil to dissolve the sugar. Simmer until the syrup thickens slightly. Add the chilli/chile, remove from the heat and leave to cool. Peel and finely dice the carrot. Scrape the seeds from the cucumber, discard, then finely dice the flesh. Roughly chop the peanuts. Add everything to the cooled chilli/chile syrup.

★ To make the fish cakes, cut the fish into large chunks and place in a food processor with the prawns/shrimp and coconut. Whizz until combined and nearly smooth. Remove the seeds from the chilli/chile and finely chop the flesh. Tip into a bowl with the blended fish mixture, spring onions/scallions, coriander/cilantro, curry paste and salt. Mix well. Divide the mixture into 8–10 evenly sized portions and, using wet hands, shape into patties.

★ Heat the oil in a frying pan/skillet over a medium heat and fry the fish cakes in 2–3 batches until golden brown, about 2 minutes on each side. Drain on paper towels and serve with lime wedges and the dipping sauce.

SALT & PEPPER SQUID
with Sansho spicy dip

THIS RECIPE, USING SPICY, CITRUSY SANSHO PEPPER, IS A TWIST ON THE EVER-POPULAR SALT AND PEPPER PRAWNS/SHRIMP SERVED IN CHINESE RESTAURANTS AROUND THE WORLD. DIP THE FRESHLY FRIED SQUID INTO THE SPICED MAYO AND ENJOY.

½ teaspoon ground Sansho pepper

2 teaspoons sea salt

65 g/½ cup rice flour

450 g/1 lb. squid, cleaned and sliced

freshly squeezed juice of 1 lemon

vegetable oil, for deep frying

for the Sansho spicy dip

115 g/½ cup good-quality mayonnaise

5 g/¼ cup Vietnamese or regular basil leaves

½ teaspoon Sansho pepper

½ teaspoon sea salt

grated zest of 1 lemon

serves 4

★ To make the dip, whisk all the ingredients together in a small bowl until well combined. Set aside.

★ In a large shallow bowl, mix together the Sansho pepper, salt and rice flour. Put the squid in another bowl and pour over the lemon juice.

★ Pour enough oil to come halfway up a large saucepan, then place over a medium–high heat until the oil starts to simmer. Alternatively, use an electric deep fryer.

★ Take a few pieces of squid at a time and toss in the flour mixture to coat. Working in batches, deep fry for 2–3 minutes until golden and cooked through. Transfer to a wire rack to drain.

★ Pile the cooked squid in a shallow bowl and serve with the dip.

CRISPY GARLIC CHIVE CHICKEN WONTONS

1 chicken breast fillet (approx. 140 g/5 oz.), finely minced/ground

4 tablespoons finely chopped fresh Chinese chives

a pinch of ground Sichuan pepper

1 teaspoon light soy sauce

½ teaspoon sesame oil

16 wonton wrappers

sunflower or vegetable oil, for deep frying

sea salt and freshly ground black pepper

for the dipping sauce

2 tablespoons Chinese black rice vinegar

1 teaspoon caster/granulated sugar

1 garlic clove, finely chopped

½ fresh red chilli/chile, finely chopped (optional)

serves 4

DEEP-FRYING THESE DUMPLINGS UNTIL THEY ARE CRISP AND GOLDEN TRANSFORMS THEM INTO A SENSATIONAL SNACK, PERFECT WITH COCKTAILS. THE CHINESE BLACK RICE VINEGAR USED IN THE DIPPING SAUCE IS AVAILABLE FROM ASIAN GROCERY STORES.

★ Thoroughly mix together the minced/ground chicken, Chinese chives, Sichuan pepper, soy sauce and sesame oil. Season well with salt and pepper.

★ Mix together the ingredients for the dipping sauce and set aside.

★ Take a wonton wrapper and put a teaspoon of the chicken mixture in the centre of the wrapper. Brush the edges with a little cold water and bring the wrapper together over the chicken to form a parcel, pressing together well to seal properly. Set aside. Repeat the process until all 16 wrappers have been filled.

★ Heat the oil in a large saucepan until very hot. Alternatively, use an electric deep fryer. Add four of the wontons and fry for a few minutes, until golden brown on both sides, turning over halfway through to ensure even browning. Remove with a slotted spoon and drain on paper towels. Repeat the process with the remaining wontons.

★ Serve at once with the dipping sauce.

1 tablespoon sesame oil

120 g/4 oz. shiitake mushrooms

1 pak choi/bok choy

1 carrot, grated

6 spring onions/scallions, finely sliced

2 garlic cloves

1–2 fresh red chillies/chiles

2-cm/¾-inch piece of fresh ginger, grated

a handful of fresh coriander/cilantro

1 pack of frozen round dumpling (gyoza) wrappers or wonton wrappers, defrosted

cornflour/cornstarch, for dusting

sesame oil, for frying (optional)

for the ginger dipping sauce

3 tablespoons dark soy sauce or tamari

2 teaspoons dark brown sugar

1 tablespoon sesame oil

2 tablespoons rice vinegar or white wine vinegar

1 garlic clove, crushed

1 teaspoon finely grated fresh ginger

½–1 fresh red chilli/chile, very finely chopped

a squeeze of fresh lemon juice

a handful of fresh coriander/cilantro, chopped

a bamboo (or other) steamer, lined with parchment paper

makes 18

VEGETABLE DUMPLINGS
with ginger dipping sauce

THESE DUMPLINGS ARE A TASTY SNACK TO SHARE WITH FRIENDS. THEY CAN ALSO BE MADE AHEAD OF TIME AND FROZEN. BUY THE WRAPPERS FROM YOUR LOCAL ASIAN STORE OR ORDER THEM ONLINE AND USE WHATEVER YOU HAVE IN THE FRIDGE FOR THE FILLING.

★ To make the dipping sauce, put all of the ingredients in a small bowl and stir until well combined.

★ To make the dumplings, heat the sesame oil in a frying pan/skillet set over medium–high heat and add the mushrooms, pak choi/bok choy and carrot. Cook for about 5 minutes, until softened. Put the cooked mushrooms, pak choi/bok choy and carrots in a food processor along with the spring onions/scallions, garlic, chilli/chile, ginger and coriander/cilantro and blitz. Alternatively, finely chop all of the ingredients by hand.

★ Dust the work surface with a little cornflour/cornstarch and put the dumpling wrappers on the floured surface. Put 1 teaspoon of the filling in the centre of each wrapper. Using a pastry brush, moisten the edges of each wrapper with a little water, then seal the edges together. Make sure that the dumpling is well sealed – if not, add a little more water to seal it. You can use your finger to frill the edge of the dumpling for decoration. Note that the uncooked dumplings will keep, covered, in the fridge, for a few hours before steaming if you don't need to cook them straight away.

★ Put the bamboo steamer over a pan of boiling water. If you do not have a steamer, cover a colander with a make-shift kitchen foil lid. Put the dumplings in the parchment-lined steamer, cover with a lid and steam for 10–15 minutes until the filling is hot and cooked.

★ For extra flavour and texture, once the dumplings have been steamed, heat a tablespoon of sesame oil in a frying pan/skillet over a high heat and fry the dumplings for 1–2 minutes, until the bottom and sides start to colour. Be careful as they colour quickly and can easily burn.

KIMCHI PANCAKE
with black garlic crème fraîche

THIS TAKE ON THE POPULAR KOREAN STREET-FOOD DISH CONTRASTS THE CHEWY-TEXTURED, CHILLI/CHILE-HOT PANCAKE WITH THE SUBTLE COOLNESS OF CRÈME FRAÎCHE, ENRICHED WITH THE MELLOW SWEETNESS OF BLACK GARLIC. KIMCHI IS A TRADITIONAL KOREAN FERMENTED RELISH, USUALLY MADE WITH CABBAGE.

100 g/¾ cup plain/all-purpose flour

½ teaspoon sea salt

3 tablespoons kimchi liquid (reserved from kimchi)

130 g/1 cup kimchi, finely chopped

1 spring onion/scallion, finely chopped

150 ml/⅔ cup crème fraîche or sour cream

3 black garlic cloves, finely chopped

1 tablespoon sunflower or vegetable oil

thinly sliced spring onion/scallion, to garnish

serves 4

★ Make the batter by whisking together the flour and salt with 100 ml/⅓ cup water into a thick paste. Stir in the kimchi liquid, then mix in the kimchi and spring onion/scallion.

★ Mix together the crème fraîche and black garlic and set aside.

★ Heat a large frying pan/skillet until hot. Add the oil and heat well. Pour in the batter, which should sizzle as it hits the pan/skillet, spreading it to form an even layer. Fry for 3–5 minutes until set, then turn over and fry the pancake for a further 3–4 minutes until it is well browned on both sides.

★ Cut the kimchi pancake into portions and serve topped with the black garlic crème fraîche. Sprinkle with extra spring onions/scallions to garnish.

for the braised pork

1 tablespoon vegetable oil

1 onion, finely chopped

2 garlic cloves, chopped

2-cm/¾-inch piece of fresh ginger, peeled and chopped

400 g/14 oz. pork belly, cut into 2.5-cm/1-inch cubes

1 tablespoon Korean soy bean paste

1 tablespoon Korean chilli/chile paste

1 tablespoon dark soy sauce

1 tablespoon rice wine or medium sherry

1 teaspoon caster/granulated sugar

300 ml/1¼ cups chicken stock or water

for the bao (Taiwanese buns)

250 g/1¾ cups plain/all-purpose flour

2 teaspoons caster/granulated sugar

½ teaspoon fast-action dried yeast

½ teaspoon baking powder

¼ teaspoon sea salt

100 ml/⅓ cup hand-hot water

50 ml/3½ tablespoons full-fat/whole milk

2 teaspoons white wine vinegar

shredded carrot and spring onion/scallion, to garnish

a large lidded frying pan/skillet or casserole dish

a steamer

makes 8

BRAISED PORK BAO

SMOOTH-TEXTURED, PILLOWY TAIWANESE-STYLE BUNS PAIR BEAUTIFULLY WITH THE GUTSY, SUCCULENT BRAISED PORK, MAKING THESE A MEMORABLY TASTY TREAT FOR GUESTS.

★ First, make the braised pork. Heat the oil in a large lidded frying pan/skillet or casserole dish. Fry the onion, garlic and ginger for 2 minutes, stirring, until the onion has softened and the mixture is fragrant. Add the chopped pork belly and fry, stirring often, until the pork is lightly browned. Add the soy bean and chilli/chile pastes and mix to coat thoroughly. Add the soy sauce, rice wine and sugar and cook, stirring, for 1 minute. Add the stock or water and bring to a boil. Cover with a lid, reduce the heat and simmer for 1 hour until the pork is tender. Uncover the pan, increase the heat to bring the liquid to a boil and cook uncovered over a medium heat, stirring often, until the sauce has considerably reduced. Set aside.

★ To make the bao, mix together the flour, sugar, yeast, baking powder and salt in a large bowl. Add in the hand-hot water, milk and vinegar and mix together to form a soft dough. Knead for 10 minutes until the dough is supple and smooth.

★ Put the dough in an oiled bowl, cover with oiled clingfilm/plastic wrap and set aside in a warm place for an hour to rise.

★ On a lightly floured surface, knock back the dough and roll to form a thick sausage. Cut into eight even-sized pieces and shape each piece into a ball.

★ Roll each dough ball into an oval, roughly 12 cm/5 inches long. Fold each oval in half over a small rectangular piece of baking parchment. Cover with oiled clingfilm/plastic wrap and set aside to rest for 20 minutes.

★ Line the steamer with oiled parchment paper. Steam the buns in batches, spaced apart, for 10 minutes or until cooked through. Handling the hot buns carefully, remove the baking parchment. Fill each bun with braised pork, garnish with shredded carrot and spring onion/scallion and serve at once.

PEA & POTATO SAMOSAS

THESE CLASSIC VEGETARIAN INDIAN SNACKS ARE EASY ENOUGH TO WHIP UP FROM INGREDIENTS THAT YOU PROBABLY ALREADY HAVE IN YOUR KITCHEN CUPBOARD AND FREEZER. MANGO CHUTNEY IS A LOVELY ACCOMPANIMENT FOR DIPPING INTO.

300 g/10½ oz. potato, diced

a pinch of sea salt

2–3 tablespoons vegetable oil

2 shallots, finely sliced

2 garlic cloves, crushed

a thumb-sized piece of fresh ginger, grated

1 teaspoon unsalted butter

100 g/scant 1 cup frozen petits pois

1 small fresh green chilli/chile, finely chopped (optional)

½ teaspoon toasted cumin seeds

1 tablespoon freshly chopped coriander/cilantro

sea salt and freshly ground black pepper

270 g/9½ oz. filo/phyllo pastry

vegetable oil, for frying

mango chutney, to serve (optional)

makes 40

★ Put the potato in a large saucepan, cover with cold water, add the salt and bring to a boil. Simmer for approximately 8–10 minutes or until soft. Drain and mash lightly.

★ Heat the oil in a frying pan/skillet, add the shallots and cook for about 5 minutes, until softened. Add the garlic, ginger and butter to the shallots and fry for another minute. Add to the potato.

★ Cook the peas, then add them to the potato mixture along with the chilli/chile, if using, cumin seeds and chopped coriander/cilantro. Season to taste.

★ Cut the filo/phyllo pastry into 23 x 6-cm/9 x 2½-inch strips and put a teaspoonful of the potato mix in the left corner. Fold the pastry over into a triangle until the samosa is sealed. Dab on a little oil to stick the last fold in place.

★ Shallow-fry the samosas for a minute or so on each side until the pastry is crisp. Drain on paper towels.

★ Serve with mango chutney, if desired.

CAULIFLOWER & KALE PAKORAS

1 small cauliflower, cut into 2-cm/
¾-inch florets

1 tablespoon sunflower oil, plus extra
for deep-frying

2 onions, thinly sliced

a bunch of kale or dark leaf cabbage,
thinly sliced

2–4 small fresh green chillies/chiles,
to taste, finely chopped

2 large fresh red chillies/chiles, finely
chopped

1 tablespoon chilli/chili powder

½ teaspoon asafoetida powder (hing)

250 g/2 cups chickpea/gram flour

2 teaspoons black cumin seeds

2 tablespoons fennel seeds

2 tablespoons dried pomegranate
seeds (anardana)

a bunch of fresh coriander/cilantro,
roughly chopped

¼ teaspoon bicarbonate of soda/
baking soda

1 teaspoon sea salt

raita, to serve

makes about 24

PAKORAS ARE EASY TO ADAPT TO WHICHEVER SEASONAL VEGETABLES YOU HAVE AVAILABLE. CAULIFLOWER AND KALE IS A GREAT COMBINATION, BECAUSE THE KALE ADDS EXTRA CRISPNESS. FENNEL SEEDS AND DRIED POMEGRANATE SEEDS PROVIDE INTERESTING POPS OF FLAVOUR. THEY KEEP WELL IN THE FRIDGE AND CAN EASILY BE REHEATED IN THE OVEN.

★ Parboil the cauliflower for 2–3 minutes, then drain in a colander and leave for 5 minutes.

★ Heat the oil in a small pan over medium heat and fry the onions for 5 minutes or until softened. Add the kale, green and red chillies/chiles, chilli/chili powder and asafoetida, and cook for 3 minutes. Set aside.

★ Sift the chickpea/gram flour into a large bowl. Toast the cumin and fennel seeds in a dry pan over medium heat for 30 seconds, stirring occasionally, to release the aroma, then add to the flour followed by the onion and kale mixture. Add 120 ml/scant ½ cup water to make a thick paste, then add all the other ingredients and mix well. The batter should have a thick porridge-like consistency, so add a little more chickpea/gram flour or water if necessary.

★ Heat the oil for deep-frying in a deep pan. Using a tablespoon, gently drop spoonfuls of the mixture into the hot oil, frying in batches of three or four. Cook until golden brown, turning halfway through to cook both sides. Remove with a slotted spoon and drain on paper towels. Serve hot, with some raita.

DUCK BREAST CHINESE PANCAKES with jammy plums

- -

THIS IS THE PERFECT DIY BAR BITE; SERVE THE COMPONENTS INDIVIDUALLY ON A PLATTER AND LET GUESTS BUILD THEIR OWN. YOU COULD ROAST A DUCK IF YOU WANT IT CRISPY, BUT IT WILL TAKE A COUPLE OF HOURS. IT'S MUCH QUICKER TO FRY THE DUCK BREAST TO SAVE ON TIME – IT'S JUICY AND EASY TO PORTION.

175 g/6 oz. duck breast

10 ready-made Chinese pancakes (about 14 cm/5½ inches in diameter)

2 teaspoons five spice mixed with ½ teaspoon sea salt

for the jammy plums

2 plums, stoned/pitted and cut into 20 wedges

freshly squeezed juice of 1 orange

1 teaspoon grated fresh ginger

1 teaspoon caster/granulated sugar

10 teaspoons hoisin sauce

½ cucumber, cut into matchsticks

5 spring onions/scallions, cut into matchsticks

makes 20

★ To make the jammy plums, simmer the plums in the orange juice, ginger and sugar for 3 minutes in a shallow frying pan/skillet until they take on a jam-like texture.

★ Take the duck out of the fridge 20 minutes before cooking. Score the skin of the duck and trim off any excess fat around the sides. Rub the five spice and salt mix all over the duck. Put it in a frying pan/skillet skin-side down and turn on the heat.

★ When the frying pan/skillet is hot and you can hear the duck start to sizzle, let it cook for 5 minutes.

★ Sear the duck on the sides and the bottom, cooking for a further 5–8 minutes, or until cooked to your liking.

★ Take the pan/skillet off the heat and leave the duck to rest.

★ Lay the pancakes flat on a chopping board and cut in half.

★ To assemble, spoon ½ teaspoon hoisin sauce on a half-pancake and arrange a piece of duck, a wedge of jammy plum and a few matchsticks of cucumber and spring onions/scallions on top. Tightly roll into a flat cone.

450 g/1 lb. chicken fillets

12 lime leaves

5-cm/2-inch piece of fresh ginger, peeled and roughly chopped

3 garlic cloves, roughly chopped

60 ml/¼ cup coconut oil

grated zest and juice of 2 limes

1 tablespoon curry powder

1 teaspoon chilli/chili powder

½ teaspoon smoked paprika

a handful of fresh coriander/cilantro leaves

12 wooden skewers, pre-soaked

makes 12 skewers

for the garlic & mango relish

flesh of 1 ripe mango

1 fresh red chilli/chile, finely diced

grated zest and juice of 1 lime

1 tablespoon grated fresh ginger

2 spring onions/scallions, sliced

1 garlic clove, finely chopped

½ teaspoon Madras curry powder

¼ teaspoon smoked paprika

60 ml/¼ cup rice wine vinegar

1 tablespoon sesame oil

2 tablespoons groundnut/peanut oil

1 tablespoon fish sauce

sterilized glass jars with lids

makes 350 ml/1½ cups

CHICKEN TIKKA BITES
with garlic & mango relish

THESE TIKKA BITES ARE ESPECIALLY WELCOME IN THE SUMMER. THROWN STRAIGHT ONTO THE GRILL OR BARBECUE, THEY ARE READY IN MINUTES. THE LIME LEAVES GIVE A DELIGHTFUL FLORAL FRAGRANCE TO THE DISH. PERFECT ALONGSIDE A JUG OF FRUITY RUM PUNCH!

★ Begin by preparing the chicken. Cut the chicken fillets into 3.5-cm/1½-inch chunks. Thread a piece of chicken onto a soaked wooden skewer, then a lime leaf, and another piece of chicken. Take another wooden skewer and repeat until you have used up all of the chicken. Place the skewers in a large shallow bowl and set aside.

★ Put the chopped ginger and garlic, coconut oil, lime zest and juice, curry powder, chilli/chili powder, paprika and coriander/cilantro leaves in a food processor. Blend until smooth.

★ Pour the curry sauce over the prepared chicken skewers, coating the meat. Cover and set in the refrigerator to marinate for 2–4 hours.

★ Light the grill or barbecue, or place a grill/broiler pan over a medium–high heat. Put the skewers directly on the heat or in the pan and cook for 4 minutes on each side, until the chicken is cooked through.

★ For the relish, cut the mango into 5-mm/¼-inch cubes and place in a bowl. Add the chilli/chile, lime zest and juice, ginger, spring onions/scallions, garlic, curry powder and paprika. Toss to combine.

★ In a separate bowl, whisk together the vinegar, oils and fish sauce. Pour over the mango mix and stir well to coat. Season with salt and chill in the refrigerator before serving. The relish will store in sterilized glass jars in the refrigerator for up to 1 week.

450 g/1 lb. pork tenderloin

fresh coriander/cilantro leaves, to garnish

for the spicy marinade

2 tablespoons rice wine vinegar

2 fresh green chillies/chiles, chopped

1 tablespoon soy sauce

1 large garlic clove, finely chopped

1 tablespoon toasted sesame oil

2 tablespoons fish sauce

2 tablespoons groundnut/peanut oil

2 tablespoons freshly chopped coriander/cilantro leaves

1 tablespoon grated fresh ginger

for the spiced peanut sauce

1 tablespoon groundnut/peanut oil

1 garlic clove, finely chopped

2 red Thai chillies/chiles, finely chopped

4 kaffir lime leaves

1 lemongrass stalk, cut into 4

1 teaspoon garam masala or curry powder

2 tablespoons dark brown sugar

225 g/1 cup peanut butter

250 ml/1 cup coconut milk

30 g/1 oz. unsweetened coconut flakes

finely grated zest and freshly squeezed juice of 1 lime

2 tablespoons fish sauce

18–20 wooden skewers, pre-soaked

a ridged griddle/grill pan

makes 18–20 skewers

SPICY PORK SATAY
with spiced peanut sauce

THESE SPICY PORK SKEWERS DIPPED IN SPICED PEANUT SAUCE ARE QUITE SIMPLY HEAVEN ON A STICK. THEY ARE ESPECIALLY GOOD WHEN YOU WANT TO MAKE DELICIOUS, EASY FOOD WITH MINIMUM KITCHEN TIME AND FUSS.

★ Slice the pork into 5-mm/¼-inch thick pieces and put in a bowl. Mix together all the Spicy Marinade ingredients and pour over the pork. Cover and put in the refrigerator for 30 minutes.

★ To make the Spiced Peanut Sauce, heat the groundnut/peanut oil in a saucepan over a medium heat. Sauté the garlic, chillies/chiles, kaffir lime leaves, lemongrass and garam masala for 2 minutes. Add the sugar and stir. Add the peanut butter, coconut milk and coconut flakes, along with the lime zest and juice. Cook for 15 minutes. Take off the heat and stir in the fish sauce. Pour the mixture into a bowl and set aside.

★ Remove the pork from the refrigerator and thread onto the soaked wooden skewers.

★ Heat the griddle/grill pan over a high heat until nearly smoking. Cook the pork skewers for 3–4 minutes each side until brown and caramelized.

★ Garnish the pork skewers with coriander/cilantro leaves and serve with the Spiced Peanut Sauce.

MELON, FIG, PROSCIUTTO & BUFFALO MOZZARELLA SALAD

PERFECT WITH A GLASS OF WINE, THIS IS A REFRESHING TAKE ON THE CLASSIC MELON AND PROSCIUTTO COMBINATION, BUT WITH THE ADDITION OF CREAMY BUFFALO MOZZARELLA AND RIPE, JUICY FIGS. ARRANGE ALL THE INGREDIENTS BEAUTIFULLY ON A PLATTER AND LET EVERYONE TUCK IN AT A LEISURELY PACE.

½ cantaloupe or charentais melon

½ galia or honeydew melon

4 fresh, ripe figs

12 slices of prosciutto di Parma

1 ball of buffalo mozzarella

a small handful of fresh mint leaves

a small handful of fresh basil leaves

freshly ground black pepper

aromatic extra virgin olive oil, to drizzle

serves 4–6

★ Carefully scoop the seeds out of the melons. Cut each melon into delicate wedges and cut away the skin. Arrange the melon wedges on a serving platter.

★ Cut the figs into halves or quarters and add to the platter.

★ Roughly tear the prosciutto and place next to the fruit.

★ Drain the mozzarella, tear into large pieces and add to the platter.

★ Scatter the mint and basil leaves over everything, season with black pepper, drizzle with olive oil and serve immediately with extra olive oil for those who want more.

PROSCIUTTO & CHORIZO CROQUETTES

50 g/3½ tablespoons butter

140 g/generous 1 cup plain/all-purpose flour, plus 50 g/scant ½ cup

300 ml/1¼ cups full-fat/whole milk

50 g/2 oz. chorizo, finely chopped

4 slices prosciutto, shredded

a big pinch of freshly chopped flat-leaf parsley

a pinch of dried chilli/hot red pepper flakes (optional)

2 eggs, beaten

75 g/generous 1 cup fresh breadcrumbs

sea salt and freshly ground black pepper

olive oil, for frying

makes 10

★ To make the croquettes, melt the butter in a frying pan/skillet and then stir in the 140 g/generous 1 cup flour. Cook for 2 minutes, then slowly add the milk, a little at a time, stirring constantly. Cook for a couple of minutes, until thick, then mix in the chorizo, prosciutto, parsley, chilli/hot red pepper flakes, if using, and some salt and pepper.

★ Remove from the heat and let cool slightly, then cover with clingfilm/plastic wrap and chill in the refrigerator for 2 hours.

★ Form the chilled croquette mixture into 10 little balls or sausage shapes. Put the remaining 50 g/scant ½ cup flour in a bowl or shallow dish. Dip your hands in the flour, pick up a shaped croqueta, roll it in the flour to coat, then dip it in the beaten eggs. Finally, coat it well in breadcrumbs. Repeat with all the croquettes.

★ Meanwhile, heat a few centimetres/inches of olive oil in a heavy-based saucepan until hot (enough to come as high as at least half the height of the croquetas). Fry the coated croquettes in the hot oil, in batches, for about 10 minutes, until they are crisp and golden all over, turning occasionally. Remove using a slotted spoon and drain on paper towels. Serve hot.

RED WINE CHORIZO

A SIMPLE RECIPE BUT ONE YOU'LL RETURN TO MANY TIMES – CHORIZO AND RED WINE ARE SUCH AN AROMATIC COMBINATION.

165 g/5½ oz. chorizo, sliced fairly thickly

olive oil, for frying (optional)

160 ml/⅔ cup red wine

serves 4

★ Heat a frying pan/skillet until hot, then add the chorizo slices and fry for 2–3 minutes, turning regularly, until they have browned on both sides and have shrunk slightly. If you have a good non-stick frying pan/skillet, you won't need oil before you put the chorizo in. If you are worried about the chorizo sticking, just add a drop or two of olive oil to the pan. The chorizo will release oils when cooked and that's the flavour you want.

★ Carefully pour the red wine into the pan over the chorizo slices and keep stirring. Cook for 2–3 minutes over a medium heat, until the red wine starts to reduce. Continue to cook until the wine has thickened and become sticky.

★ Remove from the heat and transfer the mixture to a dish. Serve.

OLIVE SUPPLI

16 cured black olives, stoned/pitted

40 g/¼ cup plain/all-purpose flour

2 eggs, beaten

140 g/scant 1½ cups dried breadcrumbs

vegetable oil, for frying

saffron salt, to sprinkle

for the risotto

20 g/½ cup dried porcini mushrooms

250 ml/1 cup white wine

500 ml/2 cups chicken stock

2 tablespoons olive oil

1 garlic clove, finely chopped

2 tablespoons fresh thyme leaves

1 tablespoon freshly chopped rosemary

200 g/1 cup arborio rice

60 g/½ cup Parmesan, grated

sea salt and freshly ground black pepper

a deep-frying thermometer

makes 16

TRADITIONAL SUPPLI HAVE MOZZARELLA INSIDE AND ARE KNOWN IN ROME AS SUPPLÌ AL TELEFONO, BECAUSE WHEN YOU BITE INTO THEM THE MOZZARELLA PULLS AND LOOKS A LOT LIKE A TELEPHONE WIRE. HIDING A CURED BLACK OLIVE IN THE CENTRE MAKES FOR A REALLY DELICIOUS SURPRISE.

★ For the risotto, soak the mushrooms in the wine for 30 minutes. Drain, reserving the liquid, and chop roughly. Pour the reserved liquid into a small pan with the chicken stock. Bring to a boil and reduce to a simmer.

★ Put the olive oil, garlic, thyme, rosemary and mushrooms in a medium frying pan/skillet and cook over medium–high heat for a few seconds, coating with the olive oil. Add the rice and stir for 2–3 minutes until well coated and translucent. Start adding the stock a ladleful at a time, stirring continuously until the liquid has been absorbed. Continue until you have used all the liquid, which should be about 20 minutes. Stir in the cheese and season with ground black pepper and salt. Pour onto a large plate and spread out to cool.

★ To make the suppli, take tablespoons of cooled risotto and form 16 balls. With your forefinger make a dent in each risotto ball and place an olive in the centre. Roll the risotto ball in your hand to reshape and cover the olive.

★ Dust the suppli balls with flour, dip into the beaten egg and then toss in the breadcrumbs until well coated. At this stage they can be left to rest in the refrigerator for up to 6 hours until you are ready to cook them.

★ Heat the oil in a heavy-based saucepan until the oil reaches 180°C (350°F) on a deep-frying thermometer. Alternatively, test the oil by dropping in a cube of bread. It should turn golden brown in about 20 seconds.

★ Fry the suppli in batches until crispy and golden brown, about 2 minutes. Drain on paper towels. Sprinkle generously with saffron salt and serve.

ROAST GARLIC SALT COD CROQUETTES
with parsley pesto

THESE CRISP, LIGHT-TEXTURED CROQUETTES, WITH THEIR SUBTLE, SALTY, FISHY FLAVOUR, ARE ADDICTIVELY GOOD. SERVE WITH THE GLORIOUS FRESH PARSLEY PESTO FOR A REAL TREAT OF A SNACK.

1 whole head of garlic

600 g/1 lb. 5 oz. salt cod fillet, soaked for 24 hours, with water changed 2–3 times during soaking period

600 g/1 lb. 5 oz. floury potatoes, such as King Edward, peeled and chopped

2 eggs, lightly beaten

2 tablespoons freshly chopped flat-leaf parsley

grated zest of 1 lemon

oil, for deep-frying

sea salt

for the parsley pesto

2 cloves of roasted garlic from the bulb (above)

50 g/2 cups freshly chopped flat-leaf parsley

120 ml/½ cup olive oil

salt

makes 24

★ Preheat the oven to 180°C (350°F) Gas 4.

★ Slice the top off the garlic head, to expose the cloves inside. Wrap in foil and bake the garlic head in the preheated oven for 1 hour. Unwrap the foil and set the garlic head aside to cool.

★ When the garlic is cool enough to handle, squeeze out the softened roast garlic from each clove. Set aside and then mash four cloves for the croquettes and two cloves for the parsley pesto.

★ To make the croquettes, drain the soaked salt cod and place in a saucepan. Cover generously with cold water, bring to a boil and cook over a medium heat until tender, around 20 minutes, then drain.

★ Boil the potatoes in salted water until tender, then drain, mash and allow to cool. Mix the four mashed roast garlic cloves into the potatoes.

★ When the salt cod is cool enough to handle, use your fingers to go through it and discard any skin and bones. Flake the fish.

★ In a large bowl, mix together the flaked salt cod, mashed potato, eggs, parsley and lemon zest, mixing well. Using 2 tablespoons, shape the mixture into 24 croquettes and set aside to cool completely.

★ To make the parsley pesto, blitz together the parsley, two mashed roast garlic cloves and olive oil in a food processor, then season with salt.

★ Heat the oil for deep-frying in a large saucepan until very hot. Fry the croquettes in batches until rich golden brown, turning them over during frying so that they brown on both sides. Remove and drain on paper towels. Serve warm from frying or at room temperature with the parsley pesto on the side.

SALT-CRUSTED CITRUS SHRIMP

with spicy dipping sauce

finely grated zest and freshly squeezed juice of 2 limes

1.8 kg/4 lbs. coarse sea salt

450 g/1 lb. large raw prawns/shrimp such as tiger prawns, unshelled

for the spicy dipping sauce

2 fresh red chillies/chiles, finely chopped

4 kaffir lime leaves, finely shredded

1 spring onion/scallion, finely chopped

1 garlic clove, finely chopped

125 ml/½ cup fish sauce

finely grated zest and freshly squeezed juice of 2 limes

1 tablespoon rice wine vinegar

1 tablespoon brown sugar

1 tablespoon peanuts, chopped

serves 4

THIS IS AN ATTENTION-CATCHING PLATE AT ANY BAR OR TABLE OF FRIENDS. CRACK OPEN THE SALT CRUST AND BE DAZZLED BY THE HEAVENLY AROMAS AND THE BRIGHT PINK SHELLS.

★ Preheat the oven to 240°C (475°F) Gas 9.

★ In a large bowl mix the lime zest and juice, salt and 250 ml/1 cup water. The mixture should be the consistency of wet sand. Spread a layer of the salt mixture in a baking dish and arrange the prawns/shrimp on top. Cover with the remaining salt mixture and pat well down, making sure the prawns/shrimp are completely covered and there are no gaps anywhere.

★ Bake in the preheated oven for 15 minutes. The salt should be slightly golden on top.

★ Whisk together all the Spicy Dipping Sauce ingredients until the sugar has dissolved. Divide between four small bowls.

★ When the prawns/shrimp are ready, take them out of the oven and leave them to rest for 5 minutes. Using the back of a knife, crack open the crust and remove the top part. Serve at the table.

★ Invite your guests to peel their own prawns/shrimp, and dip in the spicy sauce. Have a large empty bowl handy for the shells.

CHORIZO & RED (BELL) PEPPER FRITTATA BITES

4 x 60-g/2-oz. chorizo sausages

16 eggs

300 ml/1¼ cups crème fraîche or sour cream

a pinch of sea salt and freshly ground black pepper

1 tablespoon olive oil

150 g/1 cup (about 1 medium) finely chopped red onion

1 garlic clove, crushed

130 g/1 cup fresh or frozen peas

1 red (bell) pepper, deseeded and cut into strips

60 g/1¼ cups baby spinach

ovenproof frying pan/skillet

cocktail sticks/toothpicks

serves 8–10

A FRITTATA IS A THICKER OMELETTE/OMELET THAT IS FRIED BEFORE BEING FINISHED OFF IN THE OVEN. CUT INTO BITE-SIZE SQUARES, THIS ONE MAKES A FAIRLY HEALTHY AND DELICIOUS BAR SNACK.

★ Preheat the oven to 180°C (350°F) Gas 4.

★ Put the chorizo sausages on a baking sheet and cook in the preheated oven for 12 minutes. Remove from the oven, drain on paper towels and cut into 1-cm/½-inch slices. Cover and set aside.

★ Reduce the oven temperature to 110°C (225°F) Gas ¼.

★ Put the eggs in a large mixing bowl with the crème fraîche and lightly whisk to combine. Season with salt and pepper, and set aside.

★ Heat the oil in a large non-stick, ovenproof frying pan/skillet set over a low–medium heat. Add the onion and garlic and sauté until soft but not coloured. Add the sliced chorizo, peas and pepper strips and cook for 2–3 minutes, stirring occasionally. Add the baby spinach and stir until the spinach just begins to wilt.

★ Arrange the mix evenly over the base of the pan/skillet and carefully pour in the egg mixture. Reduce the heat and gently cook the frittata, moving the egg in a little from the edge of the pan as it cooks (similar to how you would cook an omelette/omelet) using a spatula to run around the outside of the pan. You don't want to get any colour on the base of the frittata so it is important to keep the temperature low. Continue running the spatula around the outside of the pan to ensure the frittata doesn't stick.

★ After about 10 minutes, once it has just set on the bottom and the sides, place the pan/skillet in the oven for 15–20 minutes, until the frittata is lightly golden and just set in the middle. Remove from the oven and set aside to cool for 10 minutes. Once cool, cover the pan with a chopping board and turn it over to release the frittata. Cut it into 4-cm/1½-inch squares and transfer to a plate to serve.

2 tablespoons butter or olive oil

1 onion, grated or finely chopped

150 g/2½ cups finely chopped chestnut mushrooms

15 g/½ oz. dried porcini mushrooms, soaked in hot water until soft, and then finely chopped, reserving the soaking liquid (optional)

1 garlic clove, crushed

grated zest of 1 lemon and freshly squeezed juice from ½ lemon

100 g/½ cup risotto rice

150 ml/⅔ cup dry white wine (optional)

300 ml/1¼ cups vegetable stock

a small bunch of fresh flat-leaf parsley

50 g/⅔ cup freshly grated Parmesan

5 mm/¼-inch cubes red (bell) pepper (you could also use a few peas or diced courgette/zucchini per ball)

500 ml/about 2 cups vegetable oil, for frying

sea salt and freshly ground black pepper

fresh mayonnaise, to serve (optional)

for the breadcrumb coating

50 g/⅓ cup plus 1 tablespoon plain/all-purpose flour, seasoned with salt and pepper

1 egg, lightly beaten

100 g/1¼ cups dried white breadcrumbs

makes 16

LEMON & MUSHROOM RISOTTO BALLS

ARANCINI (SICILIAN STUFFED RICE BALLS) ARE A GREAT WAY TO SERVE RISOTTO. THEY MAKE VERY SATISFYING BITE-SIZE NIBBLES.

★ To make the risotto, melt the butter in a heavy-based saucepan over a low heat. Add the onion and cook gently for 10 minutes, add the mushrooms and cook until softened. Add the garlic and cook for another minute.

★ Turn up the heat to medium and add the lemon zest and rice. Stir well until the rice becomes opaque. Add the white wine, if using, and stir until all the liquid has been absorbed. Add about 200 ml/¾ cup of the stock and stir until the liquid is absorbed. Add any leftover liquid from the porcini, but leave the sediment. Stir well until the liquid has been absorbed, then keep adding stock and stirring until the risotto rice is cooked, about 20 minutes. The consistency should be thicker than a normal risotto so that the balls will hold their shape. While the risotto is still hot, stir the parsley and Parmesan through it until incorporated.

★ Spread the rice on a large plate to cool it quickly to room temperature, then form it into 16 bite-size balls. To fill the balls, put each one in the palm of your hand and push down into the centre with your thumb, and put a few red pepper cubes in, then cover with the rice and roll back into a ball.

★ For the breadcrumb coating, put the flour, beaten egg and breadcrumbs in three separate bowls. Roll each ball in the flour and tap off any excess. Then roll in egg, then breadcrumbs. Set the balls aside in the refrigerator until ready to fry.

★ Pour the vegetable oil into a deep saucepan, filling it no more than halfway. Heat the oil carefully and do not allow it to smoke. It is ready when a small piece of bread takes 15–20 seconds to brown. Cook no more than four balls at a time until golden brown (1–2 minutes). Drain excess oil on paper towels, and serve warm with mayonnaise, if liked.

for the base/crust

170 g/1½ cups plain/all-purpose or wholemeal/whole-wheat flour

a small pinch of fast-action/rapid-rise yeast

1 tablespoon olive oil

a pinch of sea salt

1 teaspoon caster/granulated sugar

for the topping

1 tablespoon olive oil

300 g/11 oz. pancetta, thinly sliced or diced

400-g/14-oz. can of tomatoes, drained and chopped

a big pinch of freshly chopped parsley

a big pinch of freshly chopped or dried oregano

1 tablespoon tomato purée/paste

200 g/7 oz. pecorino or Parmesan, grated or shaved

sea salt and freshly ground black pepper

a large baking sheet, greased or lined with parchment paper

makes 6 pizzettes

PIZZETTES

THESE MINI PIZZAS ARE QUITE FILLING, SO THEY'RE IDEAL FOR SERVING WITH DRINKS WHEN YOU NEED SOMETHING A LITTLE MORE THAN A NIBBLE BUT LESS THAN A HUGE FULL-SIZE PIZZA!

★ Preheat the oven to 180°C (350°F) Gas 4.

★ For the base/crust, put all the ingredients in a bowl, add 125 ml/½ cup water and mix together with your hands to make a dough. If the mixture feels sloppy, just add a little more flour, or add a little more water for the opposite (it shouldn't be so dry that it crumbles when you roll it). Turn the dough out onto a flour-dusted surface and knead for 5–10 minutes, until smooth and elastic. The kneading is always a bit boring but just remember that you need to do it or your base will be chewy and tough. If you have a bread maker, it will do the work for you – just follow the timing instructions for your machine.

★ Divide the dough into 6 even pieces. On a flour-dusted surface, roll out each portion of dough into an oval. Place the pizza bases/crusts on the prepared baking sheet and bake in the preheated oven for 10 minutes, turning over halfway through.

★ Meanwhile, prepare the topping. Heat the olive oil in a frying pan/skillet. Add the pancetta and fry over a medium heat, until fully cooked – let it brown but don't reduce it right down at this stage because it will continue to bake on top of the pizzettes. Put the canned tomatoes, parsley, oregano and tomato purée/paste into a bowl, season with salt and pepper and mix well.

★ Once the pizza bases/crusts are initially baked, remove from the oven. Spread the tomato mixture over the top of the bases/crusts. Put the pancetta pieces on top, then sprinkle over the cheese.

★ Return the pizzettes to the preheated oven on the middle shelf (ideally, put the pizzettes directly onto the oven shelf, rather than using the baking sheet, so the bases can continue to crisp) and bake for a further 15 minutes, until the cheese has melted. Serve hot.

PROVENÇAL CRUDITÉS PLATTER 'LE GRAND AÏOLI'

THIS EXTRAVAGANZA ORIGINATES FROM PROVENCE IN THE SOUTH OF FRANCE AND IS A GLORIOUS CELEBRATION OF THE REGION'S PRODUCE. IT IS A COLOURFUL SELECTION OF TENDER YOUNG VEGETABLES, DISPLAYED ON A PLATTER AND SERVED WITH AÏOLI, WHICH IS OFTEN REFERRED TO AS 'THE BUTTER OF PROVENCE'.

a selection of raw or blanched baby vegetables, to include (bell) peppers, carrots, radishes, cucumber, spring onions/scallions, fennel, celery hearts, sugar snap peas or mangetout/snow peas, fine green beans and cherry tomatoes

eggs, hard-boiled/hard-cooked, peeled and halved

French country bread, ideally a Provençal 'fougasse'

pots of unsalted French butter

sea salt flakes

serves 4–6

★ Prepare your vegetables, a good selection of crudités should include red or yellow (bell) peppers cut into strips, baby carrots with the tops left on (or larger carrots cut into batons), radishes with stems and leaves on, cucumber (unpeeled and sliced into thick batons lengthways), trimmed spring onions/scallions, fennel (quartered and sliced), celery hearts with the leaves left on, sugar snap peas or mangetout/snowpeas, fine green beans (blanched) and sweet cherry tomatoes on the vine.

★ Serve your vegetable platter with hard-boiled/hard-cooked eggs, plenty of French country bread, ideally a Provençal fougasse or 'ladder bread' with accompanying butter and sea salt flakes, and a simple Saffron and Garlic Aïoli. Arrange the prepared vegetables on a large oval platter and serve the dip in a bowl, then let your guests help themselves.

★ To make the aïoli, put 2 room-temperature egg yolks (organic and very fresh) in a bowl and add 1 teaspoon Dijon mustard, 1 teaspoon crushed saffron threads (soaked in 1 tablespoon of lukewarm water), 1 crushed garlic clove and ½ teaspoon each of salt and black pepper. While whisking, slowly drizzle in 200 ml/¾ cup grapeseed oil until it is all incorporated. Add 1 tablespoon freshly squeezed lemon juice and mix again to finish. Cover and keep refrigerated until ready to serve.

★ To drink, opt for a Provençal rosé wine, well chilled or, if preferred, a light white, such as an unwooded Chardonnay or Sauvignon Blanc.

SEASONAL CHEESEBOARD

a selection of 5–7 cheeses of varying colours, flavours and textures

fresh or dried fruits, depending on the season

membrillo (Spanish quince preserve) or damson paste

spiced fruit chutneys and preserves

a selection of cheese biscuits/crackers, including water biscuits and oatcakes

enriched breads (such as walnut and raisin bread), optional

serves 6–10

CHEESEBOARDS ARE SIMPLE TO ASSEMBLE AND ALWAYS POPULAR. A SPECIALIST CHEESEMONGER IS THE IDEAL PLACE TO SHOP, BUT MOST SUPERMARKETS NOW CARRY A GOOD RANGE. THE BOARD IS ENHANCED BY ATTRACTIVE SEASONAL ACCOMPANIMENTS.

★ Choose a selection of cheeses with flavours ranging from creamy through to piquant, and a variety of textures too. You might like to start with a Gorgonzola or other soft blue cheese, a firm goats' cheese, such as Crottin de Chavignol, a wedge of Brie, a whole Camembert (still packaged in its attractive round wooden box), a French Comté or similar dense Swiss cheese such as Gruyère. A Spanish Manchego can be a good addition, and look out for aged or smoked varieties or a good mature/sharp Cheddar.

★ Different cheeses are complemented by both fresh and dried fruits, so offer these alongside. In spring, green apple slices, fresh herbs and baby salad leaves can be appealing, while in summer, fresh cherries and grapes work well, as do fresh figs. Come autumn/fall, pears and red apples come into their own, and in winter dried apricots, figs, Medjool dates and large Muscat

raisins all work well. Shell-on nuts are both delicious and attractive to look at on a board, especially for a festive occasion. Walnuts go perfectly with blue cheeses, salted almonds pair with hard cheeses such as Manchego, while hazelnuts and smoked cheeses are a lovely combination. Preserves are also a nice addition. Choose a fruit paste such as the Spanish quince membrillo or damson paste, or jarred preserves such as spiced apple or caramelized onion chutney, which works well with gooey French cheeses such as Camembert.

★ Arrange your cheeses artfully and garnish with fresh or dried fruit and nuts, according to the season. Let the weather guide you on drinks too. Red wine is an obvious choice, but don't be afraid to experiment. A chilled Sauvignon Blanc works very well with a goats' cheese in summer and good artisanal ciders and craft beers can also pair very well with an autumn/fall board. The key is to experiment and find matches that you enjoy, before sharing them with friends.

PIÑA COLADA JELLIES

- -

THESE HEAVENLY CUBES, FLECKED WITH CHERRY AND PINEAPPLE, ARE ALL THE BEST PARTS OF A COCKTAIL IN A MOUTHFUL. THE RECIPE MAKES 120, WHICH SOUNDS A LOT, BUT THEY GO VERY QUICKLY!

700 ml/scant 3 cups pineapple juice (not from concentrate)

34 sheets of gelatine, softened in cold water for 5–10 minutes

350 ml/1½ cups cherry juice

400 g /14 oz. sweetened condensed milk

300 ml/1¼ cups Malibu or other coconut-flavoured white rum

80 ml/⅓ cup coconut cream

25 x 18-cm/10 x 7-inch and 12 x 9-cm/4½ x 3½-inch containers, lined with clingfilm/ plastic wrap

makes about 120 cubes

★ Heat 120 ml/½ cup pineapple juice to a simmer in a saucepan. Take off the heat, squeeze the water out of 11 sheets of gelatine, add to the juice and whisk. Add this to the remaining pineapple juice and whisk. Pour into the large prepared container and set in the refrigerator for at least 3 hours.

★ Heat 60 ml/¼ cup of the cherry juice to a simmer in a saucepan. Take off the heat, squeeze the water out of 6 sheets of gelatine, add to the juice and whisk. Add this to the remaining cherry juice and whisk. Pour into the small prepared container and set in the refrigerator for at least 3 hours.

★ Once both jellies are set, heat 180 ml/¾ cup water to a simmer in a saucepan. Take off the heat. Squeeze the water out of 17 sheets of gelatine, add to the water and whisk. Add this to the condensed milk, along with the rum, 150 ml/generous ½ cup water and the coconut cream. Mix, then let cool, but don't allow it to set.

★ Cut the pineapple and cherry jellies into 1.5-cm/¾-inch cubes. Arrange the cubes in a container large enough to hold them all, then cover with the cooled coconut jelly to a depth of 2.5 cm/1 inch. Set in the refrigerator overnight. The next day, cut into 2.5-cm/1-inch cubes to serve.

BOOZY TRUFFLES WITH GINGER & CHILLI PRALINE

150 g/5 oz. dark/bittersweet chocolate, broken into pieces

for the truffle ganache

225 g/7 oz. milk chocolate, broken into pieces

90 ml/6 tablespoons double/ heavy cream

45 ml/3 tablespoons brandy

for the praline

30 g/¼ cup unsalted, skinned pistachios, roughly chopped

30 g/¼ cup blanched almonds, roughly chopped

1 teaspoon ground ginger

1 dried chilli/chile, preferably Cayenne, cut as finely as possible

90 g/a scant ½ cup golden caster sugar/raw cane sugar

small, deep, lidded container, about 1.5-litre/6-cup capacity

2 large sheets of baking parchment, one greased

a cocktail stick/toothpick

makes about 20

THE FIRST THING TO HIT YOU IN THIS DELICIOUSLY BALANCED TRUFFLE RECIPE IS THE BRANDY, THEN THE SMOOTHNESS OF THE TRUFFLE, LEAVING YOU WITH THE GENTLE WARMTH OF THE CHILLI/CHILE AND GINGER.

★ To make the truffle ganache, put the chocolate and cream in a heatproof bowl over a saucepan of gently simmering water. Do not let the base of the bowl touch the water. Stir occasionally and once melted, remove from the heat. Pour the brandy into the bowl but don't mix it! Leave to cool completely, then mix until smooth. Pour into the lidded container, seal and freeze for at least 3 hours.

★ To make the praline, preheat the oven to 160°C (325°F) Gas 3. Put the nuts, ginger and dried chilli/chile on a baking sheet, shake to mix and roast in the preheated oven for 8 minutes, or until just colouring. Put 60 ml/¼ cup water and the sugar in a heavy-bottomed pan and gently heat for about 10 minutes, or until the sugar has dissolved – don't stir, just swirl the pan to stop the sugar from sticking to the bottom. Turn up the heat and bring to a bubbling boil. Don't let it burn – you can always return the pan to the heat if it needs a little longer. Once the caramel starts to turn golden, it is ready. Add the roasted nuts to the caramel, stir to coat, then turn out onto the greased baking parchment. It will be very sticky but try to spread it with a greased knife. Leave to cool. If it doesn't start to set to a brittle consistency as it cools, return it to the pan and bring it back up to the boil – it probably just needs a bit longer.

★ Once set, crush with a pestle and mortar or a wooden spoon into small, rough pieces – they can vary in size. Transfer to a small bowl.

★ Melt the dark/bittersweet chocolate in a bowl over a saucepan, as above. Leave to cool slightly. Remove the ganache from the freezer. Scoop out teaspoonfuls, roll into a ball and roll firmly in the crushed praline. Push a cocktail stick/toothpick into the truffle and dip in the melted chocolate to coat. Use a teaspoon to help you cover the truffle evenly. Allow any excess chocolate to drip off, then place onto baking parchment and remove the stick. Let cool before refrigerating to set.

for the crumb bases

80 g/3 oz. digestive biscuits/
graham crackers

50 g/2 oz. toffee-coated
popcorn (such as Butterkist)

70 g/5 tablespoons butter,
melted

for the filling

250 g/generous 1 cup cream
cheese

250 g/generous 1 cup
mascarpone cheese

2 small eggs

1 teaspoon vanilla bean paste
or vanilla extract

200 g/scant 1 cup condensed
milk

for the topping

25 g/2 tablespoons caster/
granulated sugar

25 g/2 tablespoons muscovado
sugar

25 g/1¾ tablespoons butter

80 ml/⅓ cup double/heavy cream

50 g/2 oz. toffee-coated popcorn

*a 12-hole loose-based mini
cheesecake pan or muffin pan
(with 5-cm/2-inch holes),
greased*

12 muffin wrappers (optional)

makes 12

MINI POPCORN CHEESECAKES

POPCORN TREATS ARE SUCH A FUN AND IRRESISTIBLE SNACK IDEA. THESE MINI CHEESECAKES HAVE TINY PIECES OF POPCORN IN THE BASE AND ARE TOPPED WITH A MOUND OF POPCORN AND TOFFEE SAUCE. IF YOU USE HOMEMADE POPCORN, MAKE SURE THAT ALL THE UNPOPPED KERNELS ARE REMOVED BEFORE USING.

★ Preheat the oven to 170°C (325°F) Gas 3.

★ For the bases, crush the biscuits/graham crackers and popcorn to fine crumbs in a food processor or place in a clean plastic bag and bash with a rolling pin. Transfer the crumbs to a mixing bowl and stir in the melted butter. Place a spoonful of the crumbs in each hole of the cheesecake pan and press down firmly using the end of a rolling pin or the back of a small spoon. Retain a little of the crumb mixture to sprinkle over the cheesecakes.

★ For the filling, whisk together the cream cheese and mascarpone in a large mixing bowl. Add the eggs, vanilla and condensed milk and whisk again until smooth. Pour the mixture into the 12 holes of the pan so that they are almost full. (Depending on the size of your pan you may not need all of the mixture.) Sprinkle the reserved crumbs over the top of each cheesecake and bake in the preheated oven for 20–25 minutes until set with a slight wobble. Once cool, remove from the pan and chill in the refrigerator for several hours.

★ For the topping, heat the sugars and butter in a saucepan until the sugars have dissolved. Add the cream and heat gently until you have a thick caramel sauce. Set aside to cool.

★ When you are ready to serve, place the cheesecakes in the muffin wrappers, if using, or on a serving plate. Spoon a little of the caramel sauce over each cheesecake and top with popcorn. Serve any remaining sauce alongside for extra drizzling.

CHURROS

A CHURRO DUNKED IN THICK HOT CHOCOLATE IS A WONDERFUL WEEKEND TREAT, AND THEY GO PARTICULARLY WELL WITH TEQUILA-BASED COCKTAILS. PERFECT CHURROS COME WITH A LITTLE PRACTICE AS THE OUTSIDE SHOULD BE CRISP AND THE INSIDE CHEWY BUT LIGHT.

½ teaspoon salt

200 g/1⅔ cups white strong/bread flour

¼ teaspoon bicarbonate of soda/baking soda

260 ml/generous 1 cup water at around 70°C (160°F)

400 ml/1¾ cups sunflower or corn oil, for frying

for the dipping sauce

100 g/3½ oz. dark/bittersweet (70%) chocolate, chopped

120 ml/½ cup double/heavy cream

a cooking thermometer

a piping/pastry bag with a star nozzle/tip (optional)

makes about 30

★ Whisk the salt, flour and bicarbonate of soda/baking soda in a bowl. Add the water and whisk quite vigorously so that there are no lumps.

★ Leave to sit in the bowl for 5–10 minutes, or until cooled and thickened slightly, while you prepare the oil.

★ Heat the oil in a small saucepan and bring to 180°C (350°F). Alternatively, use an electric deep fryer.

★ Spoon the dough into a piping/pastry bag (use a star nozzle/tip if you want ridges). Twist the piping/pastry bag and hold with one hand. Gently squeeze out the dough to a 5-cm/2-inch piece and snip with scissors into the oil, frying in small batches.

★ Fry for a couple of minutes and then turn over with tongs and cook until golden brown. Drain on paper towels and keep the churros in a warm oven.

★ There is no strict shape for churros. Snipping them into the hot oil in lines is the easiest way to get started. Once you get the hang of it, you can try piping them into other shapes, such as the horseshoes shown.

★ For the dipping sauce, put the chopped chocolate in a heatproof bowl. Bring the double/heavy cream to a simmer in a saucepan, then pour over the chocolate. Let it sit for 1 minute, then stir to combine. Serve the churros immediately, accompanied by the dipping sauce.

MINI BERRY PAVLOVAS

300 ml/1¼ cups double/heavy cream

300 g/10½ oz. mixed berries, sliced into small pieces

for the meringue

red food colouring/optional

2 egg whites

a pinch of salt

120 g/⅔ cup caster/superfine sugar

for the raspberry coulis

150 g/1 cup raspberries

freshly squeezed juice of ½ lemon

1 tablespoon icing/confectioners' sugar

a baking sheet, lined with a silicone mat

a piping/pastry bag

a small paintbrush

makes 40–45

ALTHOUGH THEY ONLY TAKE 20 MINUTES TO BAKE, IT'S BEST TO LEAVE MERINGUES TO DRY OUT IN THE OVEN FOR A FEW HOURS. THEY'RE A GREAT THING TO DO AHEAD OF TIME AS YOU CAN KEEP THEM IN AN AIRTIGHT CONTAINER FOR 2 WEEKS.

★ Preheat the oven to 140°C (275°F) Gas 1.

★ If you wish to colour your meringues, paint 8 stripes of food colouring inside the piping bag from the tip, halfway up the bag. Set aside.

★ Use an electric hand-held whisk to slowly whisk the egg whites with a pinch of salt on medium speed in a clean bowl, until they are frothy. Gradually add the sugar, a teaspoonful at a time, while increasing the speed of the whisk to high. Once all the sugar has been added and the meringue is shiny, holds its shape and is not grainy, fill the piping bag.

★ Make sure there are no air bubbles. Twist the piping bag and snip the end off, 2.5 cm/1 inch from the nozzle/tip. Pipe the meringues to a diameter of 2.5 cm/1 inch, leaving a 2.5-cm/1-inch space between them. They will expand slightly when baked.

★ Put the meringues in the oven and immediately turn the temperature down to 120°C (250°F) Gas ½. It is important that you do not open the door to the oven until the meringues are baked. Bake for 20 minutes, switch the oven off and leave the meringues inside to dry out overnight or for at least 2 hours.

★ To make the coulis, place the raspberries in a small saucepan and squeeze over the lemon juice. Heat the raspberries over a gentle heat, crushing them with a fork as they heat up. Stir in the icing/confectioners' sugar. Let simmer for a minute or so, then remove the saucepan from the heat. Blend the mixture in a food processor or blender, then sieve/strain it and let cool.

★ Whisk the cream until stiff. Top the meringues with the cream and berries up to 30 minutes before serving. Drizzle with coulis just before serving.

INDEX

RECIPE CREDITS

Amy Ruth Finegold
Polenta tart with goats' cheese & tomatoes

Annie Rigg
Chicken liver parfait with fig relish & toasted brioche
Melon, fig, prosciutto & buffalo mozzarella salad
Sole goujons
Spiced fried chicken
Thai-style mini fish cakes with cucumber & peanut dipping sauce

Carol Hilker
Beer-battered onion rings
Buffalo chicken wings with homemade ranch dressing
Chicago-style baby back ribs
Deep-fried mozzarella cheese sticks
Egg rolls
Falafel
French fries
Fried green tomatoes
Maple-cured bacon & tomato sandwich
Sliders with secret sauce
Smoked chipotle wings
Spicy dill pickles
Steak sandwich with sautéed onions & blue cheese
Sweet & sour pickles
Sweet pickles
Sweet potato wedges
Ultimate grilled cheese sandwich
Vietnamese spring rolls

Chloe Coker & Jane Montgomery
Courgette/zucchini fritters with minted yogurt/dip
Lemon & mushroom risotto balls
Vegetable dumplings with ginger dipping sauce

Dan May
Boozy truffles with ginger & chilli praline
Jalapeño poppers

Ghillie Basan
Baked dates stuffed with harissa couscous
Crispy vegetables fried in turmeric batter with garlic yogurt dip
Deep-fried mussels in beer batter with garlicky walnut sauce
Deep-fried whitebait with lemon
Little spinach & feta pastries with pine nuts
Shrimp baked with tomatoes & cheese
Stuffed vine leaves

Hannah Miles
Mini popcorn cheesecakes

Jackie Kearney
Cauliflower & kale pakoras

Jennifer Joyce
Provençal crudités platter 'le grand aïoli'
Seasonal cheeseboard

Jenny Linford
Braised pork bao
Crispy garlic chive chicken wontons
Garlic & herb dough balls
Kimchi pancake with black garlic crème fraiche
Roast garlic salt cod croquettes with parsley pesto
Smoked mackerel cherry tomatoes
Tuna empanadas

Milli Taylor
Churros
Devilled eggs with shrimp
Duck breast Chinese pancakes with jammy plums
Mini berry pavlovas
Moroccan chicken puffs
Pea & pancetta crostini
Pea & potato samosas
Persian sausage rolls
Pesto vegetable crostini
Piña colada jellies
Sesame shrimp toasts

Yellow bean shrimp

Miranda Ballard
Angels on horseback
Beef & black bean sliders with corn & pepper salsa
Chorizo & scallop skewers
Cornichons wrapped in salami
Devils on horseback
Horses on devilback
Indian-style lamb sliders with minted yogurt & mango chutney
Michaelmas pie
Mozzarella pearls wrapped in prosciutto
Pizzettes
Pork rillettes
Prosciutto & chorizo croquettes
Red wine chorizo
Scotch quails' eggs
'Sushi-style' prosciutto-wrapped goats' cheese & rocket/arugula

Shelagh Ryan
Chorizo & red (bell) pepper frittata bites
Corn fritter blinis with smoked salmon & lemon cream
Crispy pork belly bites
Lamb koftes with tahini yogurt dip
Spiced mixed nuts

Valerie Aikman-Smith
Candied salted almonds
Chicken tikka bites with garlic & mango relish
Corsican olives
Empanadas with Texan hot sauce
Extra-long Hawaiian black salted breadsticks
Gold truffled potato chips
Grilled halloumi with blistered jalapeño, lime & tequila relish
Haricots verts tempura
North African roasted chickpeas
Olive suppli
Padrón peppers
Parmesan & sage wafers
Salt & pepper squid with Sansho spicy dip

Salt-crusted citrus shrimp with spicy dipping sauce
Salted pretzel bites
Southern shrimp hushpuppies with corn & poblano relish
Spiced & marinated olives
Spicy popcorn
Spicy pork satay with spiced peanut sauce
'Street hawker' tea eggs

Uyen Luu
Vietnamese chicken pies

Vicky Jones
Chickpea fritters

PICTURE CREDITS

Food photography by:
Jan Baldwin Pages 76, 79, 80, 84, 88; **Steve Baxter** Pages 50, 51, 61, 100, 116; **Peter Cassidy** Pages 20, 32, 41, 42, 47, 56, 63, 64, 69, 70, 75, 87, 94, 97, 130, 131, 135; **Helen Cathcart** Pages 22, 93, 98, 110, 112, 113, 132, 139, 140; **Georgia Glynn-Smith** Page 55; **Jonathan Gregson** Pages 10–16, 115, 120, 124; **Erin Kunkel** Pages 19, 36, 43, 67, 101, 114; **Steve Painter** Pages 24–28, 54, 60, 83, 119, 129, 136; **William Reavell** Pages 17, 89, 104; **Toby Scott** Pages 6, 38, 40, 46, 48; **Kate Whitaker** Pages 2, 8, 9, 35, 58, 90, 126; **Clare Winfield** Pages 31, 45, 53, 72, 73, 103, 107, 108, 111, 123